The Theatrical Tapes of
Leonard Thynn

D1422142

By the same author:

The Growing up Pains of Adrian Plass
The Sacred Diary of Adrian Plass (aged 37¾)
The Horizontal Epistles of Andromeda Veal

Adrian Plass
Sacred Diarist

PRESENTS

The Theatrical Tapes of Leonard Thynn

[HILTON CHURCH

Marshall Pickering

Marshall Morgan and Scott
Marshall Pickering
34 – 42 Cleveland Street, London, W1P, 5FB. U.K.

Copyright © 1989 Adrian Plass
First published in 1989 by Marshall Morgan and Scott
   Publications Ltd
Part of the Marshall Pickering Holdings Group

British Library CIP Data

Plass, Adrian
   Theatrical tapes of Leonard Thynn
   I. Title
   828′.91407

ISBN 0-551-01875-5

Text set in Baskerville by Avocet Robinson, Buckingham.
Printed in Great Britain by Courier International

Contents

This book is dedicated to:
Matthew, Joseph, David and Katy.

Who put up with their father's bad temper when he is trying to write funny stuff

dedication

Dear Reader,

Sometimes I wish I'd never collected Andromeda Veal's letters together for publication. You wouldn't believe how many people from the church have mentioned 'casually' that they've always thought their lives would make a good book. Vernon Rawlings, for instance, who's got a prefab down in Armistice Row and changes his ministry like other people change their socks, approached me with the modest suggestion that I should write his biography and entitle it *Miracle Man—The Vernon Rawlings Story.* He said he thought it would be good if the person who designed the cover made his name look as if it was carved out of massive blocks of stone. I said I'd think about it, which was a lie.

Mrs Flushpool, on the other hand, informed me regally that she was prepared to accept my assistance in the composition of a 'most important spiritual work' to be called: *Crossing the Carnal Swamp* or *Escape from the Natural.* She added that her appointed spouse, Stenneth, would contribute lengthy footnotes as he was one who, since his regeneration, had never been sucked into the bog. This was no more attractive a proposition than George Farmer's offer to supply material for a worship leaders' manual with the title: *Spontaneous Worship and How to Organise it so that it Happens the Same Every Week.*

Much more constructive, it seemed to me, was an idea put forward by Gloria Marsh, an attractive widowed lady who attends our Bible-study group from time to time. Gloria sat very close to me on the settee one evening, and said she'd been looking through her old diaries and letters and wondering if she might have some material worth publishing. She asked if I'd like to come round for a few evenings and look through her bits and pieces to see if there was anything I fancied. Anne, who must have been listening through the hatch, refused this invitation rather abruptly on my behalf. I felt that this was somewhat presumptuous and probably unscriptural. After they'd all gone, I asked Anne what was wrong with providing a little comfort to a lonely soul. She said, 'It's not her soul I'm worried about . . .' Ah, well, perhaps she's right. She usually is.

Richard Cook, round to visit one evening, said that he thought it would be a good thing to produce Christian periodicals to combat the pernicious effect of the girlie magazines that you can see (if you look, which he doesn't) on the top rack in newsagents' shops. Gerald suddenly became animated. 'Yes,' he said, 'you're right, Richard. We could publish our own magazines!'

'What would they be called?' asked Richard, stepping goofily over the precipice as usual.

'Well, one could be called *Prayboy*,' said Gerald earnestly.

Richard's mouth was hanging open to the size of a golf ball.

'And then we'd have *Amen Only*,' continued Gerald, 'and how about *Repenthouse*?'

Richard almost needed the kiss of life to jerk him back into the land of the living, and we nearly lost him again when Gerald asked if he'd be willing to remove his glasses for the centre-fold. I don't know what Gerald would do without Richard to act as his straight-man.

Richard's son, Charles, wrote to me from Deep Joy Bible School to suggest that I help him with a book

2

he felt he had to write, and which would change the face of Christian outreach as we know it. The title was to be *How to Communicate that which has been Vouchsafed to us by He Who Would Have us Share that which we have Received Through the Mighty Working of His Eternal Will, in Everyday Language, by One Empowered to Make an Open Profession of Faith to Those Who Have Ears to Hear.*

'A catchy little title,' said Gerald when he saw it.

There was also a request from Percy Brain for me to read what he described as a 'Lawrencian short story', written by his second cousin's nephew's best friend's aunt on several sheets of greaseproof paper with a blunt pencil. Percy said he wanted me to be absolutely honest about what I thought of it, because his second cousin's nephew's best friend's aunt wanted good constructive criticism and not hollow flattery. As far as I could decipher, the story was about a crowd of very odd people saying inexplicable things to each other during a sea voyage on a liner. It was full of lines like: 'She was deeply curious about her own liver . . . 'and 'She fell into his chest . . . ' At the end of the story the five main characters all fell into the sea at the same time, and found each other's true selves in a joyously deep act of drowning. When I suggested mildly to Percy Brain that his second cousin's nephew's best friend's aunt might need to do a little work on her manuscript before it was ready for publication, he revealed that, in fact, *he* was the author of the story. He said that if he had known he was to be viciously harangued by a jealous so-called fellow-author, he would never have allowed me to see what one of his closest and most unbiased friends had described as 'a modern classic'. He refused to speak to me for a fortnight.

It certainly never occurred to me that Leonard Thynn would have anything worth publishing. The only thing I'd ever seen him reading (apart from the Bible on church weekends — everyone reads the Bible on church weekends) was *The Good Pub Guide* and the *Beano*. Then, a few months ago, he invited Anne, Gerald and I round for the evening to listen to some tapes he'd made. I'd forgotten that he'd recorded most of the meetings and rehearsals leading up to the Christian drama festival that our church contributed to last year. He even recorded the evening itself, which is interesting because . . . well, you'll see for yourself as you read on. It was me who directed our 'presentation', and it was such a hectic business that while I hardly noticed Thynn's infernal machine revolving away constantly.

Anyway, after listening to all the tapes, Gerald and Anne persuaded me that this was something that should be shared with the world. I wasn't quite so sure, not least because I didn't exactly come over in the most dignified light. Thynn got so excited though, and Gerald and Anne were so sure that it would help other church drama groups (in a 'negative' way, whatever that might mean), that I gave in and agreed to transcribe and edit the tapes. I do hope it was a good idea . . . .

Yours Truly,
Adrian Plass.

One

How it all got started . . . and almost ended

After an announcement during church one Sunday, that we hoped to enter the local Christian drama festival in a few weeks' time, this meeting was intended to be a brainstorming session. All were welcome, and as free refreshments were provided, thirteen people came. Edwin, our elder, suggested that I should take the chair.

[*Tape commences with a succession of crackles and hisses as Thynn's tiny brain wrestles with the complexity of a switch that is labelled in big red letters: PRESS TO RECORD.*]

ADRIAN PLASS (A.P.): Right, well we'd better get started. We're meeting this evening to discuss . . .

THYNN: (*Interrupting.*) Hold on a sec.! I don't think it's recording. (*More crackles and hisses.*) Yes it is. Sorry! Carry on.

A.P.: We're meeting this evening to discuss . . .

THYNN: Wait a minute—the little red light's not on. I'm pretty sure the little red light ought to be on. I don't think it's recording. Yes it is! No it's not! Wait a minute. (*Tumultuous crackles and hisses and thumps, together with unseemly words mut-*

5

tered by Thynn under his breath but clearly audible on the tape.) Right, I'll just do a test . . .

A.P.: (*With rather impressive patience.*) Leonard, old chap, we really ought to . . .

THYNN: (*In a high-pitched, unnatural voice.*) Testing, testing, one two three testing! This is your sound sound-man testing for sound. One two three, I'm L.T., this is a sound test, testing for sound. One two . . .

A.P.: (*With slightly less patience.*) Leonard, I really think . . .

[*Sound of machine being switched off, followed by sound of machine being switched on again.*]

THYNN: There you are, it was recording all right after all. Let's get on. It's late already.

A.P.: (*Through his teeth.*) We're meeting this evening to discuss the . . .

THYNN: Could we just wait while I run the tape back to the beginning? There's no point in . . .

[*Sounds of a chair falling over and a forest of crackling and hissing as A.P. goes over to strangle Thynn. Repenting at the last moment he whispers in his ear instead.*]

A.P.: (*Hissing murderously.*) If you don't shut up about your tape recorder, do you know what I'm going to do?

THYNN: (*Nervously curious.*) What?

A.P.: I'm going to thread the tape up one of your nostrils and pull it down the other.

THYNN: (*After a moment's consideration.*) Fair enough. (*In normal tones.*) I don't think there's much point in running the tape back to the beginning. I'll just start recording from here.

[*Sounds of A.P. picking his chair up and sitting in his place again. Very faint sounds of THYNN whispering 'waste of tape' to himself.*]

A.P.: Right! Good! Perhaps we can get on now. We're here this evening to discuss . . .

MRS FLUSHPOOL: (*Interrupting.*) I realise that I am not the chairman of this meeting, but do you not feel that supplicatory cover is a fundamental requirement at the commencement of a Christian endeavour such as this?

[*Puzzled silence.*]

ANNE: (*Sitting next to me.*) I think Mrs Flushpool means that we ought to start with a prayer, darling.

7

A.P.: Oh! Err . . . yes, of course. A prayer. Right! Err . . . would anyone like to . . . ?

CHARLES COOK: *(Back from Deep Joy Bible School the day before.)* Shall I . . . ?

A.P.: Yes, Charles, go ahead.

CHARLES: Okay, let's just turn away from the hurly burly and the rush and bustle and the every-day concerns and the toing and froing and the ups and downs and the worries and the problems and the responsibilities and yesterday's regrets and today's anxieties and tomorrow's fears and . . .

A.P.: *(Loud throat clearing noises.)*

CHARLES: . . . and let's just get into that peaceful state where we're just ready to just receive and just listen. Let's just keep silence for just a minute while we just err . . . do that.

[*A minute's silence during which Charles can be heard making little smiley sipping noises with an occasional isolated 'just' escaping like air from a slow puncture in a bicycle tyre.*]

. . . we just want to just ask that this thing we're going to do — I can't remember just what it is just at the moment — just that it will really be just really blessed in a way that's really just right and that we'll all be really conscious of how you just want to really help us to just do it in the right way and that all those involved will just really come to know that you just want to just really show them how you really just want them to just realise the truth about just understanding that you're really err . . . just.

GERALD: *(Leaning over to whisper in my ear.)* If you don't stop him soon, dad, we're going to just have

8

three choruses and just a call to the front before we just get started.

CHARLES: So we ask that we'll just really know your will and really just be really encouraged — oh, hallelujah! *(He starts to sing.)* Bind us together . . .!

A.P.: *(Loudly.)* Amen!

[*A volley of 'Amens', ranging from the half-hearted muttering of Thynn, still preoccupied with his machine, to Vernon Rawlings' manic cry of 'Amen! Hallelujah! Bless you, Lord! Oh, yes, amen indeed!'*]

A.P.: (Wearily.) We're meeting this evening to discuss what our contribution to the . . .

ANDROMEDA VEAL (A.V.): *(Here with Uncle Edwin.)* I'm afraid I don't find that very funny.

ANNE: *(Sensing my imminent breakdown.)* What don't you find very funny, darling?

A.V.: What Mrs Plushfool said about Uncle Adrian bein' the Chair*man*.

MRS F.: *(Sitting up very straight, like a water bed standing on end.)* My name, child, is Flushpool, not Plushfool . . .

A.P.: Oh, for goodness sake . . .

MRS F.: . . . and I fail to see how a mere child such as yourself could have any comment to make on my remarks to the chairman.

A.V.: That's why I intersected—insurrected—indisected—said what I said just now. He's not a chairman, he's a chair*person*!

MRS F.: May I say, in love, little girl, that, in my view, the feminist movement is almost certainly contrary to scripture. I myself am under the authority of my husband, Stenneth. *(Sharply.)* Confirm that please, Stenneth!

9

STENNETH F.: Eh? Oh, yes, dear. Absolutely. What-ever you say . . .

A.V.: And can I say in love, Mrs Slushpoof, that I wish you'd go and live on the Isle of Person, or anywhere really, and . . .

ANNE: That's quite enough now, Andromeda. You mustn't be rude. Please stop laughing, Gerald. It doesn't help!

EDWIN: *(Mildly.)* Let's just say that we call Adrian 'Chair'. All agree?

[*Chorus of assenting murmurs.*]

A.P.: *(A pale shadow of himself.)* We're meeting this evening to discuss . . .

THYNN: Could we go back to where you said 'Oh, for goodness sake'? The little red light wasn't . . .

A.P.: *(Stands and flips his lid.)* All right! Okay! Fair enough! Let's not talk about drama. Let's talk about tape recorders and little red lights and what I ought to be called, and let's pray great long prayers and say things to each other in love! Let's not do what we came here to do! Let's completely waste our time and then eat all the food and then go home! *(Sound of a body slumping back into a chair.)*

[*Silence.*]

ANNE: *(Soothingly.)* Everyone's listening now, darling.

A.P.: *(Quietly grim.)* We're meeting this evening to discuss what our contribution to the local Christian Drama Festival ought to be. This is a brainstorming session, so I'll just write down all the ideas everyone has, then we'll discuss which is the best one to use. That's all—it's quite simple really. Quite simple. It really is.

THYNN: Excuse me, Chair . . .

A.P.: *(Very calm.)* If this is about your tape recorder, Leonard, I shall commit grievous bodily harm on your person.

THYNN: No, no it's an idea—for the festival.

A.P.: *(Guardedly.)* Yes?

THYNN: Well, it's about this man, right? He's an alcoholic, dependent on drink. Drinks all the time. First, we see him sitting at home drinking. *(Continues in a low, dramatic voice.)* He takes one drink, then another, then yet another until the bottle is empty. In the next scene we see him with a bottle of vodka. Again he drinks it glass by glass. He bemoans his fate and cries aloud for help. In the third scene, just as he drinks the last drops from a bottle of rum, he's converted, and everything's all right!

[*Pause.*]

A.P.: And may I ask, Leonard, who you thought might selflessly abandon sobriety to enact this moving piece of drama?

THYNN: Well, I thought as it was my idea, I should . . .

A.P.: I thought so. Next!

THYNN: But . . .

A.P.: I've written it down. Next!

PERCY BRAIN: *(In resonating theatrical tones.)* I believe I may lay claim to more theatrical experience than that of this whole company combined. I have considered the matter with great care, and I know what we must do. It shall be an epic! The entire history of the holy bible will unroll across the vast wooden plain of the stage. In scene after magnificent scene, we shall depict the gigantic

11

forces of creative energy flinging the sun into its place on the black cloth of heaven, the making of man and his Fall, the construction and journeying of the mighty Ark through the floodwaters of divine punishment, the tragic tale of the kings and prophets of Israel, the misery of Egyptian captivity, the parting of the waters of the Red Sea, the tale of Daniel and the gigantic image before which he would not bow, the birth, life and death of our Lord, the imprisonments, shipwrecks and mighty deeds recorded in the Acts of the apostles, and finally, superbly, cataclysmically, the visions, the battles, the judgments, and the final days of this planet, as pictured in the book of Revelation!

A.P.: It's going to be a bit hard getting all that into ten minutes.

RICHARD COOK: And we've only got thirty-one pounds, sixteen pence in the entertainment budget.

EDWIN: And we can't have proper scenery because of the different groups coming on and off stage.

GERALD: And the vast wooden plain of the stage is actually ten blocks pushed together.

A.P.: And we haven't got enough people for that sort of thing anyway.

THYNN: Apart from that it was a jolly good idea, Percy. *(Laughs immoderately.)*

PERCY: *(Glaring at me as Othello glares at Iago in the last scene.)* Am I to understand that the scenario I have laid before you is to be rejected with the same sneering contempt with which you flung a previous manuscript back into my poor smarting face . . . ?

A.P.: *(Firmly.)* I never flung anything back into your poor smarting face, and we haven't rejected your ideas, I simply tried to point out that . . .

PERCY: I sensed no carping reluctance in your manner on that occasion when you requested the loan of my excellent mechanical hedge-trimmer. Is that act of generosity and open-heartedness to be forgotten so swiftly? With what grief I echo the poet's words: 'There might I see ingratitude with an hundred eyes gazing for benefit, and with a thousand teeth, gnawing on the bowels wherein she was bred . . . !' *(Rests his head on his arms as if grief-stricken.)*

[*Depressed pause.*]

A.P.: Yes, well—can we get on? Has anyone . . .

MRS THYNN: *(Turning her hearing aid up.)* Can I ask a question?

A.P.: *(Warily.)* Yes?

MRS T.: When are we 'avin' the food, and why 'ave we got to call you Claire?

ANNE: *(Kindly but loudly.)* Not 'Claire', Mrs Thynn. Edwin said we should call Adrian 'Chair'.

13

MRS T.: *(Groping for comprehension.)* But that's sillier than callin' 'im Claire! Why 'ave we got to call 'im Chair? No one's called Chair!

A.P.: *(Almost shrieking.)* It's short for Chairman, Mrs Thynn! I'm the chairman you see!

MRS T.: Well, why aren't we callin' you Chairman then?

A.P.: *(Shrieking.)* Because Andromeda thinks we shouldn't be sexist!!

MRS T.: Why're we takin' any notice of a scrap of a girl tellin' us we shouldn't exist? Anyway, when's the food?

A.P.: *(In a little, hoarse, broken voice.)* Leonard, could you please convey to your mother that no one gets anything to eat until I get some ideas down on this piece of paper? That is what we are here for.

PERCY: *(Finding his grief ignored.)* Blow, blow, thou winter wind, thou art not so unkind . . .

GERALD: . . . as Claire's ingratitude to Percy.

VERNON RAWLINGS: *(Preventing infanticide by interrupting.)* Err . . . Charles and I have got something, Chair. We sat up late last night and worked it out. It's a sort of thing for sort of Christian outreach. It sort of came to us in a surge last night, just like it must have been in the upper room, although we were actually in the basement not that it matters, because whichever room . . .

A.P.: What was your idea, Vernon?

VERNON: Yes, well, we thought we'd write something sort of gritty and real that would really glorify the Lord and bring a mighty blessing to everyone who sees it, didn't we Charles?

CHARLES: Yes, we really just . . .

VERNON: We thought we could start with the drama festival and then move to one of the provincial theatres, and go from there to the West End before doing a year-long international tour, didn't we Charles?

CHARLES: Yes, we just really . . .

VERNON: And last night I had a dream that mightily confirmed the leading we felt! In my dream I was a dolphin performing in one of those aquarium places, and the trainer was brushing my teeth with a giant toothbrush! Wasn't he, Charles?

CHARLES: Well, I wasn't really just there . . .

A.P.: I'm afraid I don't really see . . .

VERNON: (*Very excited.*) Surely it's obvious! The performance bit's about acting—the stage, you know. The trainer's God, and he's symbolically purifying the fish—that's me, for the task ahead.

GERALD: What I don't quite see . . . apart from the fact that you do look a bit like a dolphin, Vernon, is why you should appear as a creature like that?

VERNON: That's the really *great* part of it, isn't it, Charles?

CHARLES: Yes, it's really just . . . !

VERNON: The fish is a symbol of Christianity!! Amen?

CHARLES: Halleluj . . . !

A.V.: (*Dispassionately.*) A dolphin's not a fish. It's a mammal.

VERNON: (*Carried away by enthusiasm.*) Well, what's the difference . . . ?

A.V.: The diff'rence is that fish've got cold blood and gills and fins. Mammals are aminals that (*with relish*) *give suck* to their young. I done it in a project while I was an attraction in hospital. So there!

VERNON: (*Slightly irritated.*) Well, dolphins *look* like fish!

A.V.: P'raps God doesn't know the diff'rence between fish and mammals. P'raps he's forgot, seein' as it all started millions of years ago.

MRS F.: It *all* started, as you so irreverently put it, child, six thousand years ago, and . . .

EDWIN: Come now, Victoria, don't be too dogmatic with the child . . .

A.V.: *(To Vernon.)* Why don't you ask God to do another dream tonight with you as a haddock. Haddocks are real fish, aren't they, Charles? And you look more like a haddock.

CHARLES: *(Completely confused.)* I just really don't really just . . .

A.V.: Mind you, I've never heard of haddocks performing in public.

MRS T.: Why're we talkin' about performin' haddocks, fer Gawd's sake? I thought we was choosin' a play!

THYNN: Sort that lot out, Claire!

A.P.: The next person who calls me Claire is neither going to be in the play, nor have any food.

ANNE: Come on, dear, it was only a joke. Don't be childish.

A.P.: I wasn't being childish—I was just . . .

MR F.: I think we have a fundamental doctrinal issue to settle before we proceed any further. This child . . .

A.P.: Anyone who insists on settling fundamental doctrinal issues isn't going to be in the play or have any food either.

MR F.: *(Nobly.)* Victoria will never allow threats or promises to affect her defence of scriptural puri . . .

MRS F.: Be quiet, Stenneth.

MR F.: Yes, dear.

PERCY: Alas, the gratitude of man, hath often left . . .

16

A.P.: Anyone misquoting bits of poetry about ingratitude gets no part and no food either.

[*Pause.*]

Right! *Please* can we get on. Vernon and Charles—never mind about the dream. Just tell us what your idea is please.

VERNON: Okay, well basically it's one chap talking to another chap in a pub. We thought a pub was sort of better, because it's sort of real and—well, real, and if there's anything we want to be, it's real, so we thought it ought to be in a pub, so that it's real.

A.P.: (*With grinding patience.*) Yes? And . . . ?

VERNON: One chap's a Christian called Dave and the other's a non-Christian called Bart, and they have a really natural sort of conversation about sort of faith, don't they, Charles?

CHARLES: Yes, it's really just natural, just like a really natural err . . . conversation.

VERNON: We'll sort of do what we've sort of written, shall we? It's not long enough yet, but we can easily sort of pad it out when—if we err . . . need to. I'm Dave, right? And Charles is Bart, aren't you, Charles?

CHARLES: Yes, I'm really just Bart.

[*Rustle of scripts.*]

VERNON: Right, well it starts with Bart sort of sitting on his own in the pub, sort of talking to himself. Right, Charles, whenever you're sort of ready. (*Whispers.*) I come in soon, but not sort of at the beginning . . .

17

CHARLES: *(Much clicking of the tongue and sighing.)* Blow! Huh! *(Sigh.)* I don't know! My life isn't going very well! I have had three big beakers of alcohol already this evening, and I shall probably have a lot more before I go home. Huh! *(Sigh.)* Blow! What is life really about? If only I could see some meaning in it all. I see no reason not to sin at present. I have a good mind to smoke a cigarette and be naughty with a lady. No wonder people such as I turn to a life of crime. Rootless and ignorant, we go around with the wrong sort of chap, not realising that with every step we move farther from God, about whom we know nothing. Barman, I hereby order another shandy, and I don't mean the children's sort! *(Click, sigh.)* Huh! Blow!

VERNON: *(Sounding like Baden-Powell addressing a Scout rally.)* Good evening, friend. May I sit at your table with you? I will not force my company on you, as that frequently produces a resentment that hardens the listener to attempted impartation of the gospel.

CHARLES: Something about your sensitivity attracts me, sunk though I am in the misery of godless self-absorption. Sit down if you wish. But—I say, you are a laughable person. Is that not a glass of orange squash in your hand? Ha-ha, you are not a man of the world as I am. I am on my fourth beaker of shandy, but—huh—who is counting? *(Sigh.)*

VERNON: I count it a joy to suffer your mockery, friend. I require no base intoxicant to produce the joy that springs from within. Can you not tell from the expression on my face that I draw from other wells than these? *(He smiles a ghastly, crinkly smile.)*

18

GERALD: *(Leaning over to whisper in my ear.)* If anyone smiled at me like that in a pub you wouldn't see me for dust . . .

A.P.: Sssh!

CHARLES: Now that you mention it there is an almost visible aura of joy, peace and contentment about you. To what do you attribute this phenomenon?

VERNON: No, no, friend, let us talk first about your life and work, your hobbies and interests. In this way we shall establish an easy, natural relationship—a platform on which to build a friendship that is not exclusively concerned with the welfare of your soul. Scripture supports this method of approach.

CHARLES: I am a welding person, recently made redundant. Life does not seem worth living to me at present. Blow! Huh! *(Sighs.)* I have been sitting here all evening attempting to drown my sorrows through the medium of alcohol. I have already consumed three beakers of this devil's brew. It is shandy, and I don't mean the children's sort. But enough of me. Now that we are close friends and you have shown yourself interested in me as a person and not just as a

form of spiritual scalp, tell me the origin of the love, joy and peace that flows from you like a river.

GERALD: *(Whispering again.)* Yeah! What's he put in his orange squash?

A.P.: Sssh!

VERNON: As you ask me, friend, I shall tell you. I am a Christian, and the joy that you witness is a product of redemptive suffering, apprehended through divinely implanted spiritual vision, nurtured and developed through appropriately organised exegetical study.

CHARLES: I have never heard it explained so simply. Oh, that I too might share this simple faith. *(Sighs.)*

VERNON: But you *may* share it, friend! You may indeed! You must choose now between shandy and God. Choose God and you will become as I am.

GERALD: *(Another whisper.)* Back to the shandy then, I guess.

A.P.: Sssh!

CHARLES: I abhor thee, devil drink! I choose God! *(Pause.)* The feeling of joy that I am suddenly experiencing is at once more powerful and subtle than that induced by the excessive consumption of shandy, even though it's not the children's sort. Thank you, friend, for your words.

VERNON: *(Smugly.)* Not I, friend, but he who speaks through me.

CHARLES: And what now, friend?

VERNON: Well, there's a Bible study on Monday, the church meeting's Wednesday evening, Thursday there's a new nurture group starting—you'll need to get to that. Friday night there's a coach going to hear John Wimber, Saturday there's a day-long conference on next year's mission, and Sunday it's service in the morning, Azerbaijanian meal at lunchtime, and communion in the evening.

CHARLES: Free at last!

[*Sound of two people clapping. It is Vernon applauding Charles and Charles applauding Vernon. A short silence follows.*]

VERNON: *(With shy pride.)* Well, that's it. What do you think?

A.P.: *(Clears throat.)* It—it—it's certainly very . . .

VERNON: *(Anxiously.)* You don't think it's too sort of street-level? Charles and I were a bit worried that it might be a bit too sort of street-level, weren't we, Charles?

CHARLES: Yes, we were really just a bit worried about err . . . that.

A.P.: No, I err . . . don't think you need to worry about that.

VERNON: *(Slightly hopeful.)* You don't think it comes over too raunchy and realistic?

A.P.: *(As if considering carefully.)* No, no, I wouldn't say that at all.

ANNE: *(Kindly.)* You must have both worked very hard on it I expect, didn't you?

CHARLES: Well, we just really felt that God had really just given it to us.

GERALD: *(Whispering in my ear.)* Glad to get rid of it, I should think.

A.P.: Ssh! Okay, well what did other people think?

EDWIN: Good effort. Jolly good effort! Not perhaps quite what we . . .

PERCY: As I understand it, there are a mere two characters in this—'effort', as Edwin so eloquently describes it. Are the rest of us to be 'pub extras'? If so, I strongly prot—

A.P.: *(Quite gratefully really.)* That's a very good point actually, Vernon. As Edwin said, it's a very good—a very good—a very good err . . . effort, but it does only involve two characters, so it is just a little bit limiting. Anyway, we know it's there if we want to . . .

GERALD: *(Whispering.)* Put on something really bad.

A.P.: . . . if we want to come back to it later. Now, Gerald *(thinking to teach him a lesson)*, how about you? Have you got anything to offer?

GERALD: Funny you should say that, dad. *(I might have known.)* As it happens I have prepared a little scene. Not quite as Pinteresque as Vernon and Charles' err . . . effort—more sort of observed behaviour rather than anything to do with outreach and that sort of thing.

A.P.: What sort of 'observed behaviour'?

MRS F.: *(Grimly.)* I trust we are not about to enter the realms of your accustomed flippancy, young man.

GERALD: *(Gravely sincere.)* Thank you, Mrs Flushpool. I appreciate that.

MRS F.: *(Bewildered.)* What are you thanking me for?

GERALD: For your trust, Mrs Flushpool, for your trust. Thank you for trusting me.

ANNE: That'll do, Gerald. What's your idea?

GERALD: Well, basically, it's a couple of typical young Christians meeting in one of the restaurants at one of the big Christian holiday events like 'Let God Spring Into Royal Acts Of Harvest Growth' or something like that.

A.P.: Typical young Christians?

GERALD: Yes, more or less.

A.P.: Go on then.

GERALD: Well, there's Gary. He comes from *(puts on a voice)* 'a really great fellowship in the Midlands—really lively and the gifts are used, and the pastor's written three books, and we have some really great speakers, and two of my best friends have come through in the last six months, and we've just started a prophetic basketball group, and last week we claimed Greenland for the Lord, and next year a group of us are going over there, and we've had lots of prophesies about ice melting and the summer going on right through the winter, and I'm trying to decide whether to be a full-time evangelist or a Christian scuba-diver and my prayer partner said he sees me immersed in water so I think that's quite clear guidance really, and I'm reading a great book at the moment called *Origami and the Christian—a Frank Look at what the Scriptures say about Paperfolding*, and some of us are going to go and hold up posters outside the local stationer's next Friday, and I've just written a devotional song with G minor seventh diminished in it, and . . .'

A.P.: *(Amused but nervous.)* And the other one?

GERALD: Well, about the same really, except his name's Jeremy and he's not sure whether to be a full-time Christian entertainer or a charismatic accountant. Anyway, this is how it goes. I'll have to do both parts myself because I haven't practised it with anyone. It starts in the middle of their conversation.

Jeremy: . . . so I thought it would be great to join O.M. *(Casually.)* I had a chat with Ishmael about it last time he was up.

Gary: Oh, do you know Ish?

Jeremy: Oh, yeah, Ian's a good friend.

23

Gary: Nice house—nice place to stay.

Jeremy: *(Defeated.)* You've stayed there, have you?

Gary: Well, err . . . no, not exactly stayed as such, but I've heard that it's a nice err . . . place to stay.

Jeremy: *(Relieved.)* He's great though, isn't he?

Gary: Oh, yes, he's great!

Jeremy: So what are *you* going to do?

Gary: Well, I think I might be being led to spend some time with YWAM. I heard all about it from a chap who works for C.L.C. Bumped into him up at C.B.C. when I was working for S.U. He's an A.O.G. who used to be an R.C. Made the move after a B.Y.F.C. rally.

Jeremy: Impressive, was he?

Gary: Not initially. He was introduced to me by a bloke from L.S.S.

Jeremy: Are they sound?

Gary: And light, yeah. Anyway, after this chap had talked about YWAM for a bit I really felt I was being led in that direction, so I took the whole idea to Elsie and talked it through.

Jeremy: What's that stand for?

Gary: What does what stand for?

Jeremy: L.C.?

Gary: It doesn't stand for anything. It's my girlfriend's name—Elsie.

Jeremy: Oh, I see!

Gary: What's that stand for?

Jeremy: What does what stand for?

Gary: O.I.C.?

Jeremy: Nothing, I was just . . .

Gary: Only joking! Anyway, after talking about YWAM to this chap . . .

Jeremy: The R.C. who became an A.O.G. after going to B.Y.F.C.?

Gary: Yes, that one. After talking to him and Elsie I really felt led to go and work with old Floyd again.

Jeremy: Old Floyd? You mean Floyd McClung? You mean the one who wrote that book—the one with the brown cover?

Gary: Yes, that's the one. That was a great book, wasn't it?

Jeremy: That was a *great* book!

Gary: A *truly* marvellous book.

Jeremy: Mmmm . . . what a book!

[*Reverent pause.*]

Gary: You've err . . . you have read it, have you?

Jeremy: Well—flicked through it, you know . . . You?

Gary: Not read it, no, but everyone says it's err . . .

Together: A great book!

Jeremy: What did you mean about 'working with Floyd again'?

Gary: *(Airily.)* Oh, we did a mission together a couple of years ago, that's all.

Jeremy: You and Floyd McClung did a mission together?

Gary: Well, afterwards he said he wanted to personally thank me for the support I gave him—actually he said he wanted to personally thank about a hundred and twenty of us for the support we gave him, but I always felt he gave me a special look, so . . .

Jeremy: Actually, I'm really into the music side of things lately.

Gary: Yes, I've just used G minor seventh diminished in a . . .

Jeremy: It would be great to play keyboards with someone like Martyn Joseph.

Gary: Who's he? Friend of yours?

Jeremy: *(Shocked.)* He's one of the top performers at Let God Spring into Royal Acts of Harvest Growth and Blackbelt . . .

Gary: Blackbelt?

Jeremy: Yes, it's like Greenbelt only better. Martyn's always there. He's *great!*

Gary: I think U2 are absolutely superb.

Jeremy: *(Deeply moved.)* Well, thank you very much! I didn't realise you'd heard me playing. Do you really think . . .

Gary: I said 'U2' not 'you too'. I was talking about the band called U2.

Jeremy: Oh, yeah! U2 are *really* great!

Gary: Born again Christians . . .

Jeremy: Really sort of secular as well . . .

Gary: Great music on any level . . .

Jeremy: Great how they don't act like non-Christian bands . . .

Gary: That Bono . . .

Jeremy: The things he says . . .

Gary: Really sort of honest and unhampered . . .

Jeremy: Not like a Christian at all . . .

Gary: *(Sings.)* ' . . . I still haven't found what I'm looking for . . .'

Jeremy: Great!

Gary: Great!

[*Pause*]

Jeremy: Not quite sound?

Gary: Not quite. We've found what we're looking for, haven't we?

Jeremy: We have? I mean—we *have*! Anyway, I must go. I'm meeting a girl who's here with CYPAS over by the E.A. stall. We're having tea with a U.R.C. couple who've just done a tour with M.F.O. in Africa. She's hoping to go to L.B.C. while he gets a couple of months in with W.E.C.

Gary: I think I'll have a sleep.

Jeremy: Okay, R.I.P.

Well, that's it! What do you think?

EDWIN: *(Chuckling softly.)* Extremely amusing, Gerald, but I don't somehow think it would go down too well at the local festival. They do take themselves rather seriously.

VERNON: *(Clearly puzzled.)* Of course, it's really good, Gerald, but err . . . I didn't sort of see it as funny. I mean, it was really sort of two ordinary Christian chaps having the sort of chat that, well, that we young Christian chaps have, wasn't it?

A.P.: Surely people don't really talk like that! I can't believe . . .

RICHARD: Of course they don't! We were only saying on the SPUC committee the other day, or rather a chap from SPCK was saying, that in all his years with the WCC and SASRA before that, how sensible and mature Christian conversation is, whether you're in the YMCA or a school C.U. All that stuff about initials was, frankly, completely O.T.T.

A.P.: Mmm . . . yes. I see what you mean, Richard.

GERALD: I know an A1 S.R.N. with a B.M.W. and the sweetest B.T.M. you ever . . .

ANNE: Gerald!

27

PERCY: *(Sniffing.)* Discussion is superfluous. We have already established, or I believed we had established, that a duologue is not suitable. Unless of course *(fixing A.P. with an accusing eye)* we are being abused by a nepotist!

MRS T.: *(Straining to hear.)* Who's bin bruised by a methodist? Doesn't surprise me, mind you . . .

A.P.: *(Raising his voice.)* No one's been bruised by a methodist, Mrs Thynn! Mr Brain thought I might be favouring Gerald's idea, because he's a relation!

MRS T.: I thought we wasn't doin' Revelation, like old 'Enry Irvin' over there suggested.

A.P.: *(Bawling.)* We're *not* doing Revel . . . !! Oh, never mind, Leonard, explain to your mother please.

PERCY: I will not be referred to as 'Old 'Enry Irvin' over there'!

MRS T.: Well, come an' sit over 'ere! Then you can be Old 'Enry Irvin' over 'ere!

PERCY: I have *never* been so . . . !

MRS F.: I am very much afraid that Gerald's little piece of nonsense embodies those elements of flippancy and irreverence that seem to characterise the greater majority of his utterances. I fear, Mr Chairman, that there is an undue residue of the natural in your progeny.

EDWIN: Victoria, this really is not the place for . . .

A.V.: She said 'Chairman'. She was s'posed to say 'Chair'! Somebody pass a motion—quick!

PERCY: To think that I, who once trod the same boards as—as—as Peter Butterworth, should be subjected to . . .

MRS T.: Peter Butterworth! Now yer talkin'! *(Laughs shrilly.)* 'E was in all them Carry On films, wasn't 'e? 'E was good, but my favourite was . . .

28

MR F.: *(A strange rasping laugh.)* I very much enjoyed the performances of that charming fair-haired girl who always seemed to have very large parts.

[*A profound silence falls. During it,* Mrs F. *turns with ominous slowness to look at her spouse.*]

MRS F.: I was not aware, Stenneth, that you had attended *any* of those highly questionable presentations.

MR F.: *(Even his voice is pale.)* Ah, well . . . yes, well . . . of course . . . that was—was before we were err . . . married, my dear. Before you err . . . assisted me in seeing so clearly that err . . . almost everything is err . . . wrong, as it were.

MRS F.: *(The air is heavy with 'Wait till I get you home'.)* Mr Chair . . .

A.V.: *(Interrupting with triumphant precision.)* . . . person!

MRS F.: I would like to move . . .

THYNN: Hear, hear!

MRS F.: I would *like* to move that none of the suggestions received so far be adopted. They are either ungodly, unsuitable, or incompetent.

GERALD: *(Whispering.)* And there isn't a part for her.

A.P.: Ssh! Look, could we just . . . ?

[*There is a lot of loud noise as someone crashes through the door and slams it shut behind them.*]

ELSIE BURLESFORD: *(For it is she—out of breath, but not energy.)* Hello, everybody! Hello, dad! Sorry I'm late. William and I have been at the back of the fruit shop rebuking China and doing our maths homework. William believes we can actually change the shape of countries through prayer and he's read about someone in South America who's

29

actually chipping bits off Peru, and he doesn't
see why it shouldn't happen here, and neither
do I, so we're going to . . .

GERALD: It's a great idea, Elsie! We wouldn't need
ferries to get to the Isle of Wight any more. You
and William can just stand on the mainland and
pray the island to and fro all day. Brilliant!

ELSIE: Don't be silly, Gerald. Anyway, I hope I'm
not too late, Mr Plass, because . . .

MRS T.: You 'ave to call 'im Wardrobe, love.

ELSIE: Wardrobe?

A.P.: (Shouting.) Chair, Mrs Thynn! Not wardrobe!

MRS T.: Well, I knew it was furniture . . .

ELSIE: Chair? Oh, Chair! I see! Short for chair-
person?

[*You can hear Andromeda grinning.*]

A.P.: Elsie, have you got . . . ?

ELSIE: (*Great rustling of paper.*) I've brought my idea
along. It's a poem! I thought different people
could read different verses. I've got them all
here; they've got the names on. Each person
represents a part of God's creation, you see, so
we'd all stand in a line on stage and read it out
verse by verse. What do you think?

A.P.: Well . . .

ELSIE: Let's try it out! Mr Flushpool, you're first.
Here's your verse. Off you go.

MR F.: (*Much throat-clearing. He begins to read at last in
a very small, nervous voice.*)

A lion I, a fearsome beast
I'm six feet long or more,
My teeth are white as tennis shorts
Oh, tremble at my roar.
(*Makes a tiny mewing noise.*)

30

MRS F.: Roar, Stenneth! Roar!

MR F.: *(Makes a loud mewing noise.)*

ANNE: *(Whispering to A.P.)* I say, darling.

A.P.: Yes, what?

ANNE: *(Still whispering.)* It just occurred to me that with Stenneth, Victoria and you all sitting in a line, we could do The lion, the witch, and the wardrobe! *(Dissolves into silly giggles.)*

A.P.: Sssh! Err . . . that was very impressive, Stenneth. I could just see you stalking the plains . . .

MRS T.: Why's 'e walkin' to Staines?

THYNN: Be quiet, mother. Err . . . Adrian?

A.P.: Be quiet, Leonard. Carry on Elsie, please.

ELSIE: Right! Mr Brain, you're next. It's on that piece of paper I just gave you. Start when you're ready.

PERCY: *(Declaims in a mountainous voice.)*

> An earthworm, I, a humble worm,
> Of negligible brain,
> I swallow little bits of earth,
> Then spit them out again.

(Sound of rustling paper as he searches for more.) Is *that* my *part*? That fragment of absurd doggerel? Is that *all*?

ELSIE: *(Undaunted.)* Yes, Mr Brain, it is. And it's not absurd doggerel. William's pretty sure that it's inspired verse. He's just been reading a book about a man in South-east Asia who's written fifteen full length Christian novels despite having been blind, deaf and dumb since birth. William says the things I've written are amazingly similar to the things this man's written.

GERALD: *(Whispering.)* That figures!

PERCY: Humph!

A.P.: Sssh! Not you, Percy, I was talking to Gerald.

ELSIE: *(On the warpath.)* What *did* Gerald say, Mr Plass?

A.P.: It doesn't matter what Gerald said, Elsie. Let's just carry on.

GERALD: I said . . .

A.P.: Be quiet, Gerald!

THYNN: Adrian?

A.P.: Be quiet, Leonard!

VERNON: This chap in South-east Asia sounds really sort of . . .

ELSIE: Be quiet, Vernon! Now, the next one to read a verse is Mrs Flushpool. Here you are, here's yours. You're an oak tree.

MRS F.: *(Quite flattered.)* Well, I must say that seems eminently suitable. Now, let me see . . . *(She begins reading in ringing tones that slow down to incredulity as she takes in the words.)*

An oak tree I, my arms held high,
In postures wild and cranky.
My feet beneath the stubborn sod,
My skin all brown and manky.

(Pre-natal silence.)

GERALD: Eat your heart out, Wordsworth.

A.P.: Sssh! Elsie, I'm not quite sure . . .

MRS F.: *(Faintly..)* Stenneth, defend me!

MR F.: Err . . . yes, of course, dear. Err . . . I think
Victoria is a little upset at the err . . . idea that
she has been considered physically appropriate
for this particular verse. Her skin, after all, is
not brown at all . . .

MRS F.: Stenneth!!

MR F.: Or err . . . indeed err . . . m—m—m—
manky, and we—we insist on having the err . . .
sod removed, and replaced with turf, or indeed
g—g—g—grass.

ELSIE: *(Vocal hands on hips.)* I was led to write those
words and I refuse to change a single one!

GERALD: *(Whispering.)* Stubborn little turf, isn't she?

A.P.: Sssh! Elsie, this just isn't working, is it? Perhaps
. . .

THYNN: Adrian, there's something . . .

A.P.: Be quiet, Leonard!

ELSIE: *(About to boil.)* Very well! If you don't want
what I've written, I'll tear it all up, and I'm very
sorry to have bothered you! William says that
we'll thrive under persecution, and I suppose this
is the beginning of it. This meeting is like—
like—Rumania! *(To A.P..)* I wrote a verse
specially for you, Mr Plass, and you don't even
want to hear it! William's just heard about a man
in . . .

33

A.P.: *(Surrendering.)* All right, Elsie! I'm sorry, I'm sorry, I'm sorry! I will read the verse you wrote for me and then we really must get on. Okay?

ELSIE: *(Slightly mollified.)* Well, all right then. Here it is, and you won't be all sensitive like Mrs Flushpool?

A.P.: *(Testily.)* Of course not! I shall just be objective.

ELSIE: Right, off you go then.

A.P.: *(Reads quite quickly.)*

> A slug am I, a slimy thing
> I crawl upon my belly,
> Behind I leave a sticky trail,
> My body's like a jelly.

[*Round of delighted applause.*]

ELSIE: What do you think, eh?

A.P.: *(Objectively.)* Why the blue blazes do you think I'm specially suited to read that? What is it about me that suggests a slug? I'd just like to know, Elsie!

ELSIE: Well, it had to be someone fat and humble and useful, so . . .

A.P.: *(Gritting his teeth.)* Right! That's it! Thank you all for coming! Thanks for your suggestions! Thanks for anything I've forgotten! Nothing's suitable, so we might as well all just eat all the food and clear off! If I'd had any idea that . . .

THYNN: Err . . . there's something . . .

A.P.: What?!

THYNN: It's this. This script.

A.P.: By you? I'm not interested in . . .

THYNN: No, it's by FRANK BRADDOCK. He popped in this morning and said could I bring it along because he couldn't get to this meeting. He said it's exactly ten minutes long, it's in rhyming

34

verse, and it's about Daniel in the lions' den.
It's got six characters including the narrator and
the lions and he wrote it specially for us to do.

[*Long pause while* A.P. *stares at* THYNN.]

A.P.: (*Quietly but menacingly.*) Let me get this straight,
Leonard. You have been sitting there with this
script, by a proper writer, in your pocket,
throughout this farcical meeting, during which
people have been told they have manky skins,
and bellies like jellies, and I have had to listen
to hour after hour . . .

ANNE: (*Mildly.*) Less than an hour, darling . . .

A.P.: . . . nearly an hour of unusable material; and
now, only *now* do you produce something which
might have saved us all that trouble. Is that a
fair summary, Leonard?

THYNN: Err . . . let me see . . . yes, yes, that's about
it. I—I forgot I'd got it, you see. (*Laughs hoarsely.*)

A.P.: Well, in that case I'm going to . . . (*sound of
chair legs scraping and a little scream from Thynn's
throat.*)

ANNE: You're going to forgive him, aren't you,
darling? Aren't you, darling?

A.P.: (*Breathing heavily and noisily through his nose.*) Yes!
That's it—that's what I'm going to do to you.
I'm going to forgive you, Leonard (*Barely audible
muttering*)—right in the teeth . . . (*Sits again.*)

ANNE: Is the play good, dear?

A.P.: (*Rustling of pages.*) Looks great! Just right. Listen
to this bit:
> Down in the den on the bone-strewn floor,
> Where the lost men scream and the lions roar
> Where a man whose gods are life and breath,
> Will lose his gods in the jaws of death.

[Impressed silence.]

PERCY: And are there—is there a part for, well, for . . . ?

A.P.: I should think you'd make an ideal King Darius, Percy.

PERCY: *(Beaming audibly.)* Ah! Well, that seems—yes!

MRS T.: I think if we don't get some blinkin' food soon, we ought to vote in a new chest-of-drawers to get things movin'!

A.P.: Good idea! I'd quite happily give way to a new chest-of-drawers. Right! We've got a play. I'll sort out who's playing what and allocate the other jobs like prompter and so on, then we'll have another meeting. Okay, everyone?

[Murmurs of hungry acquiescence.]

THYNN: Here, it's a good job we're finishing now.

A.P.: Why?

THYNN: Because I've almost run out of . . .

[Click! as tape runs out.]

Two

Smoke gets in our eyes

That first meeting left me a bit shell-shocked, as you can imagine, but when I got home later and had a proper look at Frank's play I felt quite encouraged. It was just right. Anne and Gerald went off to bed saying silly things like 'Goodnight Mr De Mille', and I stayed up to work out the cast list for 'Daniel in the Den'. Earlier, during the meal, I'd promised Andromeda that I'd give serious consideration to her suggestion that the play should become a modern parable, entitled: 'Daniella in the Working Men's Club', but—well, I ask you! Anyway, after a lot of thought, this was the list I finally came up with.

Narrator	—	Gerald Plass
Daniel	—	Edwin Burlesford
King Darius	—	Percy Brain
Servant	—	Elsie Burlesford
First lion	—	Charles Cook
Second lion	—	Vernon Rawlings
Third lion	—	Stenneth Flushpool
An angel	—	Victoria Flushpool
Director	—	Adrian Plass
Treasurer	—	Richard Cook
Prompter	—	Leonard Thynn
Costumes	—	Mrs Thynn & Norma Twill

Technical effects	—	William Farmer
Make-up	—	Gloria Marsh

Andromeda was not available on the date of performance, for which I sent up a brief but profoundly sincere prayer of thanks. I'm very fond of Andromeda but she is a very powerful presence when you're trying to *do* things.

As for Stenneth being a lion, well, I know he didn't put up much of a show when he read Elsie's lion poem, but I sensed how much he wanted to be in it, and besides, it occurred to me that the bit where Victoria, as an angel, had to get the lions to shut their mouths would have a very natural feel about it—in Stenneth's case anyway.

The following day I rang young William Farmer to check that he was happy to be responsible for technical effects. Happy wasn't the word! He started raving on incomprehensibly about smoke machines and coloured gels and mirror balls, whatever they might be. I just agreed with everything he said, and promised to send him a script and let him know when the next meeting was.

Surprisingly enough it was Anne who suggested I should ask Gloria Marsh to do the make-up. She said that Gloria needed to be involved and would be very useful because she'd done professional make-up once. I find Anne's attitude to Gloria oddly inconsistent. She seems to have a particular insight about which of Gloria's quite frequent requests for assistance I should respond to positively. At other times she will actually insist that we help with things I hadn't even noticed. Once, quite inexplicably, Anne and Gerald collapsed in helpless laughter after I came away from the phone to say that Gloria was asking for help in lifting a very large chest. Most odd . . .

However, I digress. I did visit Gloria on the evening following that first meeting, and she was very pleased to be asked to help. She sat me down in front of a mirror and demonstrated on my face the kind of make-up she would use. It seemed to me rather bright and garish, but Gloria said it would look quite different under stage lights. We had a very pleasant coffee together after that. She really is a sweetly ingenuous person. As I left she squeezed my hand just as a child might do with her daddy, and asked if I'd forgiven her for being a naughty girl when she borrowed our car last year and bashed it.* Naturally, as a Christian, I forgave her wholeheartedly and agreed to her request to borrow it again next week. As I walked into the Coach and Horses on my way home I felt an unusual lightness of spirit as a result of this encounter. As Ted, the barman, pulled my usual half-pint of bitter, I said whimsically, 'I feel different, Ted.' He stared at me for a few moments then said, 'Come out the closet, 'ave yer?' It was then that I realised with alarm that I was still wearing my make-up. Needless to say, when I arrived home *very* shortly after that, Anne and Gerald and Leonard Thynn nearly died laughing when I told them what had happened.

Anyway, I'd got my list sorted out, and that was the important thing. The next morning I photocopied the script and the list on a machine at work, and sent off copies to all the people involved. I also added a note to say that there'd be a meeting of the non-acting participants on the following Monday evening, and that's what the next tape is mainly about. It doesn't start with that meeting, though. You see, every Monday evening at about half past six, Leonard gets dragged along by his mother to a rather obscure

---

* See: *The Sacred Diary of Adrian Plass.*

religious group called The Ninth Day Specific Bulmerites—Baroness of Wertley's Involvement. On this particular evening Leonard had his tape-recorder with him ready to come on to the 'Daniel' meeting afterwards, and he must have pressed the record button by accident, just as the 'message' started. I wasn't going to transcribe it, but Gerald said he thought it was too wonderful to leave out . . .

[*Tape opens with the same crackles and hisses as the last one, followed by the typical coughs, shuffles and mutterings of a waiting congregation.*]

PREACHER: *(In a flat, monotonous, rather burdened voice.)* There are so many lessons to be learned in a garden.

CONGREGATION: *(Equally flatly.)* Ah, yes, in the garden. Amen, yes we witness to that etc.

P.: Only the other day I was trimming the privet that separates our garden from the next, and chatting uncommittedly to a non-Christian neighbour, when my ladder collapsed . . .

CONG.: *(Sympathetically.)* Amen, brother . . .

THYNN: Ha, ha! I mean—amen, brother.

P.: As I lay writhing on the rockery I realised, with a little spasm, that I was being taught a very important lesson. Namely, that we must expect to lose support if we start hedging.

CONG.: Amen! Thank you, Lord! Yes! etc.

P.: Recognising the providential nature of this revelation, I fetched a wooden box from the garage and, having once more ascended, re-engaged Mr Studeley in conversation. This time I was much more direct. 'Mr Studeley,' I announced, firmly, 'we are all suffering as a result of the Fall.'

CONG.: Amen! Yes! Ah! etc.

P.: '*I'm* not,' replied Mr Studeley, 'but you're bleedin' in three places.' I was about to correct his interpretation of my statement when, unfortunately, the box on which I was standing gave way with a loud crack like a pistol shot and I must have disappeared from Mr Studeley's view with quite startling suddenness.

THYNN: Hallelujah! Praise the Lord! (*Frowning silence.*) I mean—Amen, brother . . .

P.: Honesty compels me to admit that as I fell backwards onto the rockery once again, I very nearly succumbed to a recurrent temptation to ascribe randomness to the events of my life. However, seeing Mr Studeley's face appear above the privet hedge at this point, I realised that here was an ideal opportunity to show joy in adversity. Abandoning my heretical impulses . . .

CONG.: Praise God! Yes!

P.: . . . and baring my teeth in a joyful smile, I sang the following words whilst attempting to convey that I was spreadeagled in a divinely ordained sort of way. (*Sings in a flat, joyless manner.*)

> I'm H – A – P – P – Y
> I'm H – A – P – P – Y
> I know I am
> I'm sure I am
> I'm H – A – P – P – Y

Mr Studeley said, 'Banged yer 'ead, did yer? Must 'ave!' As he withdrew, I turned my eyes away from the privet hedge, and there, less than one inch from my face, was further justification for my descent. It was only a humble slug, but— and this was the point—behind it lay a shining trail. What a graphic picture of the Christian life!

CONG.: Amen! Hallelujah! We want to be slugs for you! etc.

P.: A little later, as my wife cleaned and bandaged my wounds, I said to her, 'Wife, you are a slug among women!' She stopped bandaging and said, 'In what way, pray, do I resemble a slug?' 'It is the slime!' I cried affirmingly, 'It shines!'

CONG.: Amen! Let it shine! Let the slime shine! etc.

MRS THYNN: *(Very loudly.)* As 'e started yet?

THYNN: *(Very loud whisper.)* Turn your hearing-aid to 'T', mother, you've missed half of it!

MRS T.: Oh, good, there's only 'alf to go then.

P.: My wife is a trained nurse, so I trust there was some excellent reason why she tied my left wrist to my right ankle, and my right wrist to my left ankle before leaving rather abruptly. Bent double, I hobbled out into the garden again with little shuffling steps, and balanced carefully at the edge of the lawn to await further revelations. Mr Studeley's face appeared over the hedge again. He said, 'I was just wonderin' if you was feelin'—why are you touchin' your toes? 'Ere! Your arms an' legs is all tied together! 'Oo did that then?' Suddenly inspired, I replied, 'I am in the strings of healing, whereas you are bonded to your iniquities.'

'Too right!' said Mr Studeley, 'specially first thing in the mornin' when I get out of me bed an' try to stand up. Bonded to me iniquities, I am. Couldn't 'ave put it better meself!'

MRS T.: *(Very loudly.)* 'As 'e finished yet?

THYNN: *(Loud whisper.)* I'm not sure!

P.: I was unable to resist a slight feeling of depression as Mr Studeley disappeared again; particularly as a large apple fell heavily on the back of my head at that instant. A moment's reflection, however, showed that once again a heavenly message had been vouchsafed to me. I smiled in grateful comprehension as a larger and even heavier apple hit my head, and I toppled slowly over sideways into the rockery. I knew without doubt that my efforts with Mr Studeley would be crowned with much fruit. Amen.

CONG.: *(Frenzied response.)* Hallelujah! Amen! Oh, yes! Let there be much fruit! He toppled, he toppled! Crown his efforts! Amen! etc.

P.: We now sing number seven hundred and fifty-two in the *Ninth Day Specific Bulmerites—Baroness of Wertley's Involvement Songbook*; 'Let us rush around with . . .

[*Tape clicks off*]

(Not only did Thynn not realise he'd turned his machine on and off during his hour with the Bulmerites, but when he came on to the Daniel meeting he forgot to take the pause button off until we were several minutes into the proceedings. That's why it starts in the middle of me shouting at Mrs Thynn. Also present were Leonard, Richard Cook, William Farmer, Gloria Marsh and Norma Twill, who had agreed to supervise costumes. Norma is a very pretty, single girl in her mid-twenties, who works in a factory making those pink and white marshmallows, not that it matters where she works, or that she's pretty, of course. I just mention it for information . . .)

[*Tape begins abruptly as Thynn realises he's forgotten to switch on.*]

A.P.: *(Shouting.)* I did not say 'I rely on sin', I said 'hire a lion skin'! Why on earth would I say that I rely on sin, for goodness sake? All we want you

43

to do is go along to the theatrical costumiers and hire three lion outfits! Three lion outfits! That's all!

MRS T.: I think gorillas is more frightenin'. I 'ad a dream once where this big 'airy . . .

A.P.: Lions, Mrs Thynn! It's got to be lions!

MRS T.: Oh, well, you're the Bureau, you know best I s'pose.

RICHARD: Cheap!

MRS T.: Eh?

RICHARD: Cheap! Cheap!

MRS T.: Why's 'e doin' canary impressions?

THYNN: He's not, mother! He's saying the costumes can't be too expensive!

A.P.: We're not quite as badly off as we were, because Edwin has redirected some church funds towards this project. We haven't got money to chuck about, but we should be all right if we're careful. *(To MRS T..)* All we want you to do, Mrs Thynn, is make sure those three costumes are ordered and ready to be collected when the time comes! All right?!

MRS T.: All right, I'm not deaf!

NORMA: And you want the others in black tops and tights or trousers, Adrian, is that right?

A.P.: That's absolutely right, Norma. That's exactly it, and thank you for being here and taking such an invaluable part in the proceedings. Yes, black tops and tights or trousers. After all, we want to be original, don't we? Your own clothes are, if I may say so, Norma, extremely original and attractive, just as you are yourself.

NORMA: *(Blushing audibly.)* Err . . . thank you. Do the black things have to have any special feature, or . . . ?

RICHARD: Cheap!

MRS T.: Oh, give 'im some birdseed, someone!

A.P.: The answer to your very intelligent question, Norma, is that, beyond the fact that we can't afford to be too extravagant as Richard points out, the black clothes can be plain and simple and err . . . plain. Is that okay? I do want you to feel absolutely relaxed and happy about the responsibilities that you've so kindly agreed to undertake for us. Thank you again for—well, for just being here with us. Is your chair quite comfortable? Perhaps mine would be . . .

NORMA: No, I'm fine, thanks—really.

A.P.: Well, if it gets uncomfortable, just let me know and we'll exchange seats.

THYNN: My seat's not comfortable. Let's swop . . .

A.P.: Be quiet, Leonard, we've got a lot to get through. Don't make a fuss. Now . . .

GLORIA: I'm really looking forward to seeing Mr Brain in black tights.

[*Pause as everyone mentally envisages Percy Brain in black tights.*]

A.P.: Mmmm! Perhaps you'd better jot down 'trousers' next to Percy's name, Norma, after all . . .

THYNN: We don't want to scare people off before they even see the lions, do we?

A.P.: After all, trousers look just as nice as err . . . tights. Now . . .

GLORIA: As for the prospect of seeing Victoria Flushpool in an angelic body-stocking, well, my cup runneth over.

THYNN: So will the body-stocking.

A.P.: Be quiet, Leonard. Err . . . Norma, perhaps you'd better organise a slightly err . . . fuller

45

garment for Mrs Flushpool. I'm so sorry to mess you about. Thank you for being so patient and . . .

GLORIA: I'd *love* to see *you* in tights, Adrian! Wouldn't you, Norma?

NORMA: Well, I don't—I mean, of course it would be—I mean . . .

GLORIA: He's got the figure for it, hasn't he? You have you know, Adrian. Oh, I say, I haven't said something naughty, have I? You will forgive your little Gloria if she's said anything to offend you, won't you? (*Puts on a little-girl voice.*) Big smacks for naughty-warty Glorbags if daddy's cwoss wiv her!

A.P.: (*Overcoming paralysis.*) Err . . . Daddy's not cwoss wiv—I mean, I'm not cross with you, Gloria. Err . . . could we talk about make-up?

GLORIA: Oh, yes, of course. (*Suddenly business-like.*) Well, I don't think Gerald and Edwin and Elsie and Mr Brain will need more than basic stage make-up, so that's no problem. I've got a bit myself, but I suppose we can buy more if we need it?

A.P.: Oh, yes, as long as it's . . .

RICHARD: Cheap! Cheap!

MRS. T.: D'you know, I reckon if we spent enough time, we could teach 'im to talk.

GLORIA: And the lions obviously won't need anything, so that brings us to the only real problem.

A.P.: Which is . . .?

GLORIA: How do we make Victoria Flushpool look like an angel?

WILLIAM: Why did you cast her in that part, Mr Plass?

A.P.: (*Miserably.*) It was a choice between telling her she wasn't in it, telling her she was playing a

46

lion, telling her she was playing a man's part, or letting her be the angel. *(Manfully honest.)* I'm afraid . . . *(Sigh.)* . . . I chickened out.

THYNN: *(In sympathetic tones.)* You took the lily-livered, yellow-bellied path of abject, cowardly, pathetic refusal to face the clear path of duty. Well, who are we to judge?

A.P.: *(Coldly.)* Thank you, Leonard.

THYNN: Yes, it's good to know that a Christian brother is able to openly confess that he's a wretched, snivelling, fainthearted worm of a . . .

A.P.: All right, Leonard, that'll do—thank you very much. Can we get back to the point? How do we make Mrs Flushpool into an angel? Was that the question?

THYNN: Job for Wimpey's if you ask me.

A.P.: We don't ask . . .

NORMA: *(Quite stern.)* That's very unkind, if you don't mind me saying so, Mr Thynn. In fact it's very unkind even if you *do* mind me saying so. The way to make Mrs Flushpool into an angel is not just to do with clothes and make-up; it's to do with loving and caring and saying nice things, and not always trying to placate her and shut her out by making fed-up faces about her behind her back. When was the last time any of us went round to see Mrs Flushpool when we didn't actually have to? How many of us really know what goes on inside her head; what hurts her and frightens her and excites her and makes her unhappy? She's a very difficult woman. I know that. Of course I do. But I also know that Jesus never made anyone angelic by ignoring them unless he had no choice, or by saying rotten things about them when they weren't there, and neither will we!

47

[*A long, stunned silence.*]

A.P.: Well . . .

NORMA: (*Very embarrassed.*) I – I'm sorry, I shouldn't have said all that. I had no right . . .

A.P.: (*Quietly.*) I'm very glad you said it, Norma.

THYNN: Mmm . . . wish I hadn't said that about err . . . thingy

WILLIAM: Yeah! Well said, Norms!

GLORIA: A spot of number two, you think, Norma?

A.P.: Make-up, you mean?

NORMA: (*Softly.*) I think Gloria's talking about the commandments, Adrian.

A.P.: Ah!

RICHARD: Certainly, some of our responses to Victoria have been somewhat . . . cheap.

MRS T.: I'm goin' to give you a little bell an' a ladder for Christmas, Richard. (*Pause.*) Prap's we ought to be a bit nicer to the old frump—try anyway . . .

[*Short silence.*]

A.P.: Perhaps we could move on to you, Leonard.

THYNN: (*Fiddling with his machine.*) Eh? Oh, yes! Me. I'm the prompter, you know.

A.P.: You're sure you can handle recording and prompting at the same time?

THYNN: (*Considers for a moment.*) Yes! Yep! No problem there.

A.P.: And you still want to do it?

THYNN: (*As though slightly hurt.*) Of course I want to do it! I *am* the prompter.

A.P.: So you're quite confident?

THYNN: Yep!

A.P.: No problems?

THYNN: No, none!

A.P.: Good! Great!

THYNN: Just one little thing . . .

A.P.: Yes?

THYNN: What does a prompter do?

A.P.: *(Seething.)* He lies on the floor while the director jumps up and down on his head, Leonard. Do you honestly have no idea at all what a prompter does?

THYNN: *(Vaguely.)* I thought it was a sort of soldier.

A.P.: Why on earth . . . ?

THYNN: Well, when I was about seven and at big boys' school . . .

A.P.: Big boys' school, yes . . .

THYNN: I went along to the first rehearsal of this school play that Miss Glanthorpe was doing . . .

A.P.: Miss Glanthorpe, yes . . .

THYNN: I *loved* Miss Glanthorpe!

A.P.: Get on, Leonard!

THYNN: Well, I was a bit late getting there because I had to visit the boys' tiddler room on the way— that's what we used to call it, you see.

A.P.: Really! How interesting . . .

GLORIA: So sweet!

THYNN: Anyway, when I got to Miss Glanthorpe's classroom, she said, 'Ah, Lenny, you *must* be a little prompter if you want to take part in my play,' then she gave me a soldier's uniform to put on, so I thought . . .

NORMA: You thought it meant a soldier?

THYNN: Yes. Doesn't it?

NORMA: *(A little weepy.)* I think that's a lovely story. I can just picture little Lenny trotting along to be in the play and getting all excited when he was given his soldier's uniform to wear. Oh, Leonard . . .

49

GLORIA: And thinking a prompter was a soldier. Sweet!

WILLIAM: *(Shouting.)* So did you go and see Leonard playing a soldier in the school play, Mrs Thynn?!

MRS T.: Eh? Oh, yes, I went all right! 'E was the best one in it. Better than Hoity-toity Vera Ashby-Jones' youngest, Alfred. 'E threw up just as is mother clicked 'er camera. Lovely picture that must 'ave been. He-he!

THYNN: What is a prompter, then, if it's not a soldier?

A.P.: A prompter, Leonard, is someone who sits at the side of the stage with the script in front of him, ready to help people when they forget their lines.

THYNN: *(Mentally digesting.)* I see . . . . But, in that case, if Miss Glanthorpe wanted me to be a prompter and help people with their lines . . .

A.P.: Yes . . . ?

THYNN: Why did she dress me up as a soldier?

A.P.: No, you don't understand. When she said she wanted you to be a little prompter she meant— look, I'll explain afterwards, all right? Just as long as you understand what you've got to do in the play. *Do* you understand?

THYNN: I sit at the side of the stage . . .

A.P.: On the left . . .

THYNN: I sit at the side of the stage on the left, and I've got the script in front of me, and when people forget their lines, I help them . . .

A.P.: By calling out clearly the first few words of the next line.

THYNN: . . . by calling out clearly the first few words of the next line.

A.P.: *(Relieved.)* Good! You've got it!

THYNN: Yep!

A.P.: Good. Now, Richard, let's . . .

THYNN: Just one thing . . .

A.P.: Yes?

THYNN: When do I get my uniform?

A.P.: *(Wildly.)* I've just explained! You don't . . .

NORMA: *(Kindly.)* Leonard, dear, you don't need a uniform to be a prompter—just ordinary clothes, that's all.

THYNN: *(Sounding terribly disappointed.)* I was looking forward to the uniform. I like uniforms. I haven't worn a uniform for nearly . . .

NORMA: Adrian, couldn't Leonard wear a soldier's uniform? I'm sure I could get one quite cheaply and it doesnt really matter, does it? I mean, it doesn't, does it?

A.P.: Of course, Norma, I respect your judgment tremendously but it's not . . .

GLORIA: *(Wheedlingly.)* Daddy let Lenny be a big soldier just to please his little Glorbags?

WILLIAM: Go on, Mr Plass! Say Leonard can have a uniform. Go on!

A.P.: *(In a hair-clutching sort of voice.)* I find it very difficult to believe that we are sitting here discussing what kind of costume the *prompter* should wear!

THYNN: *(Miles away.)* I *loved* Miss Glanthorpe . . .

[*Silence as several pairs of reproachful eyes bore into A.P.*]

A.P.: *(A broken man.)* All right, Leonard can wear a soldier's uniform. Why not? Why should we be rational?

[*General noises of approval and satisfaction*]

GLORIA: *(Whispering.)* Big kiss for daddy afterwards for being such a huge big kind jelly-baby!

A.P.: *(Alarmed.)* Err . . . that won't be necessary, Gloria, thank you very much. Now, if we could turn to finance just for a moment. As you know, Richard has kindly agreed to act as our treasurer for the duration of this project, using funds placed in the newly established Entertainment Budget. Richard has opened a special account at one of the local banks for this purpose, and I believe they've now sent you a cheque book, Richard, is that correct?

RICHARD: The bank in question has indeed now furnished me with a cheque book appropriate to the account in question, and I am therefore in a position to make withdrawals from the said account as and when the demand arises, and according to the way in which the Lord shall vouchsafe knowledge of his guiding will.

MRS T.: Eh?

THYNN: He says the boodle's on tap, mother.

RICHARD: On the contrary, Leonard. The 'boodle' is not 'on tap'. We have, after recent additions, the sum of seventy-five pounds in the aforesaid account, and I am entrusted with the stewardship of that sum. Last night, in a dream, I believe that I received a warning regarding the dangers of unworthy expenditure. I would like to share it with you now.

A.P.: Must it be now? We haven't really . . .

RICHARD: *(In prophetic tones.)* I saw, as it were, an mighty herd of aardvarks flying in formation through the sky. And, behold, an voice spake unto men saying, 'Touch not these aardvarks, beyond that which shall be needful to thee for thine own sustenance, for these are mine own aardvarks set aside for mine own use.' And as I watched and marvelled, some men did with mauve bows and arrows fire at and fetch down sundry aardvarks for their own sustenance and that of their kinfolk, but a goodly multitude remained and, behold, there was in this no condemnation. Then, one standing by said, 'Wherefore should we touch not these aardvarks beyond that which shall be needful for our own sustenance? Behold there existeth quite a market in aardvark skins, not to mention the attractive little knick-knacks you can make out of their teeth and so on.' And this one did then fire his arrows in mighty numbers until it did seem to rain aardvarks, and great was the falling down thereof, until they did lie as an mighty blanket upon the land, and no aardvarks flew as in the latter times. And the same voice spake saying, 'Where are mine aardvarks, set aside for mine

53

own use? Wert thou not content to take only those aardvarks needful to thee for thine own sustenance? Wherefore hast thou taken those aardvarks which were mine own aardvarks, set aside for mine own use?' Then he that spake did wax exceeding wrath, and did cause a plague of green jerbils to afflict he who had sinned. I then awoke after a short further dream about getting into a bath full of Smarties wearing a Batman costume.

[*Stunned silence, during which you can sense A.P. thanking his lucky stars that Gerald's not here.*]

A.P.: Well . . . I'm sure we shall all take to heart that warning not to waste a single aardvark—I mean, a single pound. Thank you, Richard. Our watchword shall be . . .

RICHARD: Cheap! Cheap!

MRS T.: 'Oo's a pretty boy, then?

A.P.: Okay! All requests for expenditure should come to me first, then, if I approve it, you go to Richard for the cash. Any problems? No? Good! William, you've been sitting there patiently since we started. Let's come to you now. Edwin's taking responsibility for general stage-management, props and all that sort of thing, so basically you're in charge of sound and any special effects that you can dream up.

WILLIAM: Great! Err . . . you didn't mention lights. What about the floods and the spots and the gels and the mirror-ball and the strobe and the fresnels and the follow-spots and the baby spots . . .

A.P.: I'm sorry, William, but apparently there's a sort of phantom of the opera type down at the hall,

who crouches over the lighting board all day—
and all night for all I know—and does a sort of
Incredible Hulk act if anyone else even mentions
touching it. We can send him a script and some
suggestions, but that's about it. So it's just sound
and effects, I'm afraid.

WILLIAM: That's a shame. Elsie and I have just read
a book about a man in South-east Asia who saw
two thousand people converted every week just
through the lighting arrangement in his theatre
and we thought . . .

A.P.: *Just* sound and effects, William . . .

WILLIAM: Ah, well, never mind, I could make up a
really good soundtrack with stuff like thunder
and roaring, and we could do some effects like
smoke, and people sort of glowing and—and
things.

A.P.: Exactly! Now, I think the best way to go about
this is if I read the whole thing through, and you
can talk about any ideas you've had as we go
along. Is that okay, William?

WILLIAM: Great! Great!

A.P.: Right. Well, it starts with King Darius coming
to the front of stage and addressing the audience.
Here goes:

Darius: Though ruling, ruled by men with . . .

WILLIAM: I see smoke here! Thick, curling gouts of
smoke almost obscuring the figure of the king!

A.P.: Err . . . right, I'll make a note of that. I'll start
again, shall I? I didn't get all that err . . . far,
did I? Right, here goes again—

Darius: Though ruling, ruled by men with
hooded faces,
Jealous, not for me, but for their honoured
places.

55

Lions indeed, made vicious not by hunger's
    pain,
But by their lust for power and selfish gain.
No darker hour than when I lightly penned,
This blind agreement to destroy my servant-
    friend.
Within the veil of vanity my foolish eyes,
Perceived my greatness, but could not perceive
    their lies.
Oh, God of Daniel, guard your son tonight,
Do not defend the law, defend the right.
No sleep for me, no calm, no peace, no rest,
For I have sanctified the worst, and sacrificed
    the best.

Then Gerald comes on, and Darius moves over
to the side looking all tragic and preoccupied,
and Gerald says . . .

WILLIAM: I'd see this as a moment when the—the
tragedy of the moment would be best underlined
by thunder—and smoke! Lots of grey,
mysterious smoke creeping across the floor of the
stage, really err . . . mysteriously!

A.P.: *(Doubtfully.) More* smoke?

WILLIAM: Oh, yes! Really effective!

A.P.: Mmmm . . . Well, anyway, we can come back
to that. As I said, Gerald comes to centre-stage
and speaks. He's the narrator.

Narrator: Pain is sharper than remorse,
    Death more final than regret,
    Darius will mourn tonight,
    But live his life, perhaps forget.
    While Daniel faces fearful hurt,
    Beneath the dark remorseless flood,

56

That flood of fear which runs before
The tearing down of flesh and blood.

Then, Gerald gestures behind him, and the light comes up just enough—if we can get the phantom of the opera on our side, that is—to reveal three lions sort of roaming around in the half-light, just growling softly. No sign of Daniel yet. Darius turns his head and watches the lions, and Gerald does his next bit, only it's a different rhythm—more intense and a bit faster . . .

Narrator: Down in . . .

WILLIAM: Can I cut in a moment?

A.P.: Yes?

WILLIAM: I've just had an idea.

A.P.: What is it?

WILLIAM: Smoke!

A.P.: Smoke again?

WILLIAM: Yes, as the tension gets going, so we release evil clouds of black smoke to show the satanic influences that . . .

MRS T.: I don't know why we don't just set fire to the blinkin' theatre an' 'ave done with it. Plenty of smoke then . . .

GLORIA: Aaaah, don't laugh at William's idea. I think smoke is a wonderful idea, Willy, darling.

WILLIAM: *(Blushing loudly.)* Well, I just thought . . .

A.P.: All right, it's all written down. Black smoke— right. Now, Gerald's next bit . . .

Narrator: Down in the den on the bone-strewn floor,
Where the lost men scream and the lions roar,
Where a man whose gods are life and breath,

Will lose his gods in the jaws of death.
Where the strong alone will hold their creed,
In the tearing grip of the lions' greed.

Darius: *(Turning towards audience.)*

Oh, Daniel, Daniel! save me from my
madness.
Pray your God's compassion on my sadness
Bid him send an all-forgiving rain,
To cool the fiery furnace of my brain.

WILLIAM: A quick thought! Rain on fire equals
steam, right? We could do that using . . .

A.P.: Smoke?

WILLIAM: Yes! How did you know?

A.P.: Lucky guess, I suppose. Right, now the servant
comes in. That's Elsie. She's only got a little bit
to say, but it's just as important. She goes over
to her master, Darius, and speaks to him:

Servant: I wait upon you master as you bade me
wait,
To bring intelligence of Daniel and his fate.
Some moments past, without complaint, or
sign of care.
I saw your servant thrown into the lions' lair.

Darius: Save him God, he is yours!
Save him from the lions' jaws!

Then Darius collapses onto his knees and more
or less stays there, praying, until later on, and
the servant goes off to see if there's any more
news. Then we see Daniel, played by Edwin,
coming slowly onto the stage, and he just sort
of stands there looking at the lions with his back
to the audience, while Gerald says his next bit:

Narrator: Now the moment, now the test.
See Jehovah's servant blessed,

58

As he stands, a trusting child,
Before these creatures of the wild.
Glad to pay the highest price,
To make the final sacrifice.

Now, at this stage, the lions really wake up and start to look a bit menacing—prowling around in a hungry sort of way, looking at Daniel as if he might make a good square meal. Now here, William, we really could do with a lot of . . .

WILLIAM: Smoke?

A.P.: Well, I was going to say—a lot of genuine lions' roars on tape. I don't think Stenneth and Vernon and Charles are going to keep their credibility if they start bleating out unconvincing roaring noises all over the place. But as well as that we could do with some really dramatic . . .

WILLIAM: Smoke! Right on!

A.P.: . . . some really dramatic thunder effects.

WILLIAM: Oh . . .

A.P.: That'll build up the atmosphere of danger and imminent death.

WILLIAM: Look, can I just shove a token in the fruit-machine and see if it comes up grapefruits?

A.P.: Err . . . yes. I suppose so . . .

WILLIAM: I just wondered (*As if it hasn't been mentioned up to now*) what you thought about smoke at this point. With the roaring and the thunder, *and* a sort of angry, swirling curtain of yellowish-black smoke it would be really atmospheric, wouldn't it?

A.P.: A bit of smoke might be appropriate here, William, but we do actually want the audience to be able to see what's happening on stage, don't we?

WILLIAM: Oh, sure! Yes, of course! Smoke here, then—I'll mark it off on my script. Great!

A.P.: Now, the roaring and the thunder . . .

WILLIAM: And the smoke . . .

A.P.: . . . and the smoke, yes; they go on for a minute or two while Daniel sinks quietly onto his knees, facing the audience this time, and he's obviously praying quite calmly while death comes at him from behind, as it were. Then the noise goes down a bit while Daniel speaks:

> Daniel: Lord of exiles, friend in strife,
>   In your hands I place my life.
>   Yours to take and yours to give,
>   Let me die, or let me live . . .

A.P.: Then Daniel bows his head and waits to be . . .

MRS T.: Eaten.

A.P.: Err . . . eaten, yes, or whatever, but just then . . .

NORMA: Ooooh, Adrian, it's quite exciting, isn't it?
It makes me go all shivery, the thought of lions
suddenly attacking me. Doesn't it you, Gloria?

GLORIA: Ooooh, it does!

A.P.: Anyway, just then . . .

THYNN: D'you think it's true?

RICHARD: Is what true?

THYNN: Daniel and the lions and all the rest—the
fiery furnace and all that. D'you think it's true?

A.P.: I wonder if we could postpone . . .

RICHARD: *(Deeply shocked.)* Of course it's true,
Leonard! The story of Daniel is a part of holy
Scripture, the inspired word of God. Jesus
himself quoted scripture and . . .

WILLIAM: I've just been reading about a man from
Mauritius who was converted by a semi-colon
in Leviticus! Every single jit and tattle . . .

THYNN: Jat and tittle, isn't it?

NORMA: I thought it was tat and jottle . . .

GLORIA: I thought it was ti . . .

WILLIAM: Every single little bit is there because it's
supposed to be there, and that's that!

RICHARD: The authority of scripture is absolute. It is
an unshakeable rock!

THYNN: So you're not allowed to even wonder if it's
true or not, then?

GLORIA: Oh, ye . . .

RICHARD: No!

NORMA: *(Shyly.)* I think we're allowed to wonder anything we like, really. Edwin always says . . .

THYNN: *(Remembering.)* Oh, yes . . .

NORMA: Edwin always says that the Bible is a letter
from God to us. He says it starts 'Dear Norma—
or Richard—Or Gloria', and finishes 'Love,
God', and that God meant it all to be in there,
whatever you think about it.

RICHARD: Mmmm . . . lets a few liberals in I suppose. The Bible's the Bible, in my view!

THYNN: My cousin, Finnegan Thynn, spent a year secretly smuggling Bibles *out* of China before he told someone what he was doing and they put him straight. He was amazed at the miraculous way the guards didn't notice what he was carrying, and when . . .

GLORIA: Lenny, sweetheart, I think we're telling little porky-pies, aren't we?

MRS T.: 'Course 'e is! Can't imagine a Thynn bein' that stupid! I think the Bible's a good . . .

A.P.: Do forgive me for interrupting this fascinating theological discussion, but there is a little matter of a play to be attended to, and we haven't finished yet.

[*Murmured 'sorries' etc.*]

WILLIAM: Can I just . . .?

A.P.: No, William, I'd really rather you didn't. As I was saying a very long time ago, just then, just as Daniel finishes saying his bit, and the roaring and thunder . . .

THYNN: And smoke!

WILLIAM: Thank you, Leonard.

THYNN: Don't mention it, William.

WILLIAM: I appreciate it.

THYNN: Really, it was . . .

A.P.: The roaring and the thunder and the . . .

A.P./THYNN/WILL: Smoke.

A.P.: . . . increase in intensity, until a figure enters the lions' den from the side, and that's Mrs Flushpool as the angel. She moves slowly among the lions, touching each one on the head as she goes, and as she touches them they settle down and purr like cats. So the roaring and thunder die away completely until everything's quiet. Then Daniel stands up, turns to the angel, and says . . .

WILLIAM: The smoke stays, then?

A.P.: Sorry?

WILLIAM: You said the thunder and roaring dies away, but you didn't mention the smoke. I think it's a great idea to keep the smoke. We could have gentle, soothing, everything's-all-right sort of smoke, couldn't we? It could be . . .

A.P.: *(Quietly.)* William?

WILLIAM: Yes?

A.P.: Don't be silly.

WILLIAM: Right . . .

A.P.: *(Muttering to himself.)* Everything's-all-right sort of smoke! Honestly! *(Normal tones.)* Daniel stands up, turns to the angel, and says:

Daniel: Now indeed I sing your praises,
Now indeed all terror flees,
For I see your sovereign power,
Even over beasts like these.

And the angel answers him:

Angel: God's own servant, fear me not,
Love and joy and peace are yours,
God has sent his holy angel,
I have closed the lions' jaws.
Here they lie, those mighty killers,
Harmless where great harm has been,
Sleep and when the dawn has risen,
Tell the king what you have seen.

Then the angel wafts off, and everything goes dark—Incredible Hulk permitting—and then the

63

lights come up, and the lions and Daniel have gone, and there's just Darius there, calling out to Daniel.

Darius: Servant of the living God, hear my anguish!
　Has he kept his hand upon you in your danger?
　Does your God have power to rescue you from danger?
　Daniel, speak to me!

Then Daniel appears:

Daniel: Live for ever mighty king,
　God's own angel took my part,
　Evil has no power to harm
　People who are pure of heart.
　He subdued your hungry lions,
　On their heads he laid his hand,
　So it is you see your servant,
　Happy now before you stand.

Then the last speech is from Darius:

Darius: Such a God deserves a people,
　And I vow it shall be so,
　Every soul within this land,
　Shall kneel and praise the God you know.

And that's it! Thunderous applause, we win the prize, and we all go home. Okay?

[*Pause.*]

THYNN: I really, really *loved* Miss Glanthorpe . . .
GLORIA: Jot and tittle! That's it! Jot and tittle! Got it!

A.P.: *(Suspiciously.)* You have been listening to the play, haven't you?

NORMA: *(Earnestly.)* Oh, yes, Adrian, and it's really good! Mr Braddock is ever so clever. We've all enjoyed hearing it ever so much.

A.P.: Well, thank you, Norma, and I've enjoyed . . .

MRS T.: 'As 'e finished readin' that mouldy old play yet?

WILLIAM: It's not a mouldy old play, Mrs Thynn. It's absolutely great! I'm going to ring up Stage Gear and book a smoke machine as soon as I get home!

A.P.: *(Hastily.)* We haven't actually agreed on exactly where we're going to have smoke, have we, William? Do bear that in mind, won't you?

WILLIAM: Of course! Don't worry, I'll make sure there's enough smoke.

A.P.: That's not quite—oh, never mind now. I'll ring you up later to talk about it. Everyone else quite clear?

[*Chorus of 'yes', 'yep', 'fine' etc.*]

MRS T.: '*Ow* many tiger skins?

A.P.: *LION* SKINS!! THREE *LION* SKINS!! OKAY?!!

MRS T.: That's what I thought—no need to get difficult, I'll gettem!

A.P.: Good! Norma? Richard? William? Gloria? Leonard? Questions? Problems? No? Right, I'll let you all know when the next meeting is. Thanks for coming.

[*Rustling of paper and noise of farewells until only A.P. and THYNN remain. THYNN is making a sort of snuffling noise.*]

A.P.: *(Gently.)* Leonard, what's the matter? You're not . . . ?

THYNN: M – M – M – Miss G – G – G – Glanthorpe! I m – m – m – miss her!

A.P.: *(A bit out of his depth.)* But, Leonard, that was years and years ago. She must be . . .

THYNN: She used to tell me I was good at things. I liked that. I'd forgotten . . .

[*Long pause.*]

A.P.: Errr . . . shall I pray with you, Leonard?

THYNN: To God, you mean?

A.P.: Err . . . yes, to God.

THYNN: Yes, please.

A.P.: All right, well let's turn the tape off first.

THYNN: Oh, yes, I'd forgotten about . . .

[*Click! as tape-recorder is turned off.*]

Three

A giraffe called Mr Hurd

That second meeting wasn't too bad, but it left me
with one or two misgivings. William clearly saw the
whole thing as a sort of continuous smoke-screen,
interrupted from time to time by actors peering
through the fog searching for an audience to deliver
lines to. I had an awful feeling that if I wasn't very
firm with Master Farmer the production would be
more appropriately entitled 'Daniel Gets Lost', or
'Daniel in the Smoke Den'.

My other concern was about Mrs Thynn. Her
incredible capacity for getting hold of the wrong end
of the stick (a capacity inherited to an almost clone-
like extent by Leonard—I'd seen no reason to doubt
the Finnegan Thynn story) could prove a problem,
simple though her task was. Other than that, I was
quite pleased. I even began to indulge in little day-
dreams where people shook me by the hand after the
performance and said things like, 'This is undoubtedly
a major contribution to the world of Christian drama.'
Then I'd say things like, 'Really, I had very little to
do with it,' and they'd smile at me, rather impressed
with my quiet modesty, and know that, actually, I
was absolutely *central* to the whole project. It was a
very pleasant, warming sort of picture. If I'd known
what was really going to happen I'd have booked my
passage with Gerald's friend, Gary, and gone off to

do something feasible like converting Greenland. Not having the gift of foretelling the future, however, I pressed on quite optimistically.

Leonard asked me if I'd come round the next evening so that we could practise 'being a prompter' and that's where this next tape, a shorter one, was made. When I arrived, he said that he'd just recorded a prayer about the production, and would I like to hear it? This was it.

THYNN: *(Shouting.)* I'm just going to do some recording, mother!

MRS T.: *(A distant voice, probably in the kitchen.)* All accordin' to what, Leonard?

THYNN: *(Louder.)* No, mother! I said I'm about to record on tape!

MRS T.: Can't afford to escape what?

THYNN: *(Almost screaming.)* I'M RECORDING SOMETHING! PLEASE DON'T DISTURB ME!!

MRS T.: Bees don't disturb *me* either, specially when there aren't any, like there aren't 'ere. Are you goin' loony, Leonard?

THYNN: *(Actually screaming.)* I'M RECORD . . .!! Hold on, I'll come through there . . . *(Very faint muttering as he goes.)* It'd only be about six years with good behaviour . . . *(Speaks loudly in the distance.)* Mother, I'm going to do some recording: Would you mind not disturbing me?

MRS T.: 'Course I don't mind. Why didn't you say so?

THYNN: *(Muttering again as he returns to the living room.)* I *did*, you deaf old—person. *(Sound of door closing.)* Right, now I can get down to prayer. Sitting or kneeling? I think I'll sit. After all, we're not supposed to make pointless rules for ourselves.

(Creak of armchair springs followed by a pause.) On
the other hand there's nothing wrong with
kneeling down, and maybe it's big-headed to
think I can sit, when people who're better than
me are kneeling . . . *(Sound of armchair creaking
again as Thynn kneels down. Pause.)* I don't know
though—Edwin said the other day that being
comfortable's the main thing, and my legs go
to sleep when I kneel for a long time. Think I'll
stand. *(Pause and slight huffing and grunting noises
as Thynn gets to his feet.)* This is silly! I can't relax
while I'm standing up. Maybe I could kneel on
the floor and put my head on the armchair—
no, I'll fall asleep if I do that. P'raps if I squat
on the floor with my back to the wall . . .

MRS T.: *(In the distant distance.)* Adrian's goin' to be
'ere soon! 'Ave you got through yet?

THYNN: *(Creak of springs as Thynn sits in armchair.)*
Sorry, God! I'd better get on with it or there'll
be no time left. It err . . . it's me again, God.
Thynn—Leonard Thynn, thirty-five Postgate
Drive, just past the King's Head and second on
the left as you go round the pond. I err . . . I
hope my position's all right—not too err . . .
relaxed or err . . . arrogant. I could kneel if you
like, or squat, or hang over the back of my chair
with my head on the floor, or anything really.
I hope you don't mind me bothering you again,
but I feel a bit err . . . funny, so I thought I
would. Bother you, that is. Got a bit upset
yesterday thinking about—thinking about—well,
thinking about Miss Glanthorpe and when I was
small and all. Got thinking about things. Me.
Things in the past, God. About never doing
much—being much. Got thinking about the old
hooch—booze—drink—alcohol. Haven't done

69

too badly lately, God. Almost forgotten what the inside of the old King's Head looks like. I always go the long way round to avoid Wally's off-licence. Haven't had a drink for a while. Not that I don't want one! Oh, *God* I want one! Get a bit cross with poor old mother sometimes, too. Suppose you couldn't sort her ears out—do us all a favour? No, well, up to you, of course, just a thought . . . Anyway, the point is, I don't want to be a—a Jonah in this Daniel thing. You remember Jonah? Sorry, silly question. 'Course you knew him—friend of yours. Your whale too, presumably. None of my business, naturally. I just don't want to mess it all up for the others by not being—not being—I don't know . . . good enough, or something when I'm being a soldier—prompter I mean. So, if you could sort of look after everybody who's in it, and make sure what they do doesn't get messed up by what I do, if you see what I mean, and if my uniform could be a—a good one, that would be err . . . good. And I'm sorry I said that about Mrs Flushpool and Wimpey's, and err . . . that's about it for now I think, God. Thank you for listening. Amen.

[*Click! as recorder goes off, followed by click! as* THYNN *switches to 'RECORD' after playing his prayer to me.*]

THYNN: Sounds a bit silly played back, doesn't it?
A.P.: It doesn't sound silly at all, Leonard. Better than most of my prayers. I seem to just flip tiddly-winks up most of the time. I hope I don't mess up what everybody else does as well.
MRS T.: (*From the kitchen.*) D'you want coffee, Adrian?
A.P.: (*Shouting.*) Yes please, Mrs Thynn!

MRS T.: D'you want coffee, Adrian?

A.P.: *(Bellowing.)* Yes please, Mrs Thynn!! Two sugars!!

MRS T.: D'you want coffee, Adrian?

A.P.: *(Trying to inject politeness into apoplexy.)* YES PLEASE! TWO SUGARS!

MRS T.: 'Ow many sugars?

A.P.: TWO!!

MRS T.: I'll bring the sugar through then you can 'ave what you like.

A.P.: *(Weakly.)* Thank you . . .

THYNN: Right, let's get on with the prompting practice.

A.P.: Okay, Leonard. Now, let's see . . . you sit over on that chair as though you were sitting at the side of the stage, and I'll stand in the middle of the room as if I was acting. Got your script?

THYNN: Yep!

A.P.: Good! I've got one too, so we're all set.

THYNN: *(Sounding very alert and business-like.)* Right!

A.P.: Now . . .

THYNN: We'll just pretend I've got my uniform on, shall we?

A.P.: Err . . . yes, all right, Leonard. Now, let's imagine that I'm Percy Brain playing King Darius.

THYNN: Right.

A.P.: And I've just come on stage right at the beginning of the play. I'm feeling very nervous . . .

THYNN: So am I, don't worry.

A.P.: No, I don't mean *I'm* feeling very nervous. I mean I'm pretending to be Percy Brain and *he's* very nervous.

THYNN: *(Intelligently.)* Ah, right! With you . . .

A.P.: The curtain's up and the audience is waiting for me to start. With me?

THYNN: Yep!

A.P.: So, off I go *(rustle of script)* Ready?

THYNN: Ready!

A.P.: *(A vaguely Brain-like impression.)*
Though ruling, ruled by men with hooded faces,
Jealous, not for me, but for their honoured places.
Lions indeed, made . . . err . . . made . . . err . . .
made err . . . *(Pause.)* Leonard, why aren't you
telling me what the rest of the line is?

THYNN: I don't need to.

A.P.: *(Blankly.)* Why not?

THYNN: Because you've got a script. You can look for
yourself.

A.P.: *(With rising hysteria.)* But that's because we're
pretending! On the night Percy *won't* be holding
a script—he'll have learned his lines!

THYNN: He won't need prompting in that case, will
he?

A.P.: BUT IF HE'S NERVOUS, YOU ID . . . !

[*A.P.'s raging interrupted by bumps and clatters as
MRS T. enters with the coffee.*]

MRS T.: 'Ere you are, nice cuppa coffee! 'Ow's it
goin'?

THYNN: Adrian says Percy Brain's going to forget his
lines on the night, mother.

A.P.: No I did *not* say that! Percy Brain forgetting
his lines is purely hypothetical.

MRS T.: I agree, specially at 'is age. Anyway, I'll
leave you to get on with it.

[*Bumps and door-slam as MRS T. exits*]

A.P.: Perhaps I haven't made it quite clear, Leonard.
Shall we go through it slowly again?

THYNN: *(Confidently.)* Okay!

A.P.: On the night when we do the play, Percy Brain—it could be anyone, but we're using him as an example—might get very nervous and forget his lines, even though he's actually learned them and got them in his head. Right?

THYNN: Yep!

A.P.: So you're there to help when that happens. If someone starts a line and can't remember the end of it, you're the one who reminds him or her what it is. If they can't remember how a speech starts, they'll probably say 'PROMPT', then you'll know they need help. Understand?

THYNN: Got it!

A.P.: *(Lacking faith.)* Really?

THYNN: Yep! If they forget their lines, it's up to me!

A.P.: Good! Now, let's have another go. That great big china giraffe on the wall unit's going to be the audience, right?

THYNN: Right! He's called Mister Hurd because . . .

A.P.: So I come on, pretending to be Percy . . .

THYNN: Pretending to be King Darius.

A.P.: Yes, and I, or rather, *he*, is very nervous.

THYNN: Right!

A.P.: Script ready?

THYNN: Script ready!

A.P.: Know what to do?

THYNN: Firing on all cylinders, Sah!

A.P.: Err . . . right, here we go then:
Though ruling, ruled by men with hooded faces.
Jealous, not for me, but for their honoured places,
Lions indeed, made vicious not by hunger's pain,
But by their lust for power and selfish gain.
Err . . . err . . . Prompt!

[*Rustle of script and creak of chair springs as Thynn stands up and, watched with dumb disbelief by* A.P.,

73

moves to the centre of the room and addresses the china giraffe with loony sauvity.]

THYNN: Good evening, Mister Hurd. My name's Leonard Thynn and, as you can tell by my uniform, I'm the prompter. Now, Percy's having trouble getting started on the fifth line, so I'm here to help him out. Percy, the line you're looking for is: 'No darker hour than when I lightly penned'. See you later Mister Hurd, whenever anyone's nervous, in fact. Remember: Thynn's the name, prompting's the game! Goodnight and God bless until we meet again!

[*Thynn returns to his chair, waving to the giraffe as he goes. A.P. stands, silently transfixed, for quite a long time.*]

THYNN: *(Modestly.)* I thought those extra bits up all on my own.

A.P.: *(A little, quiet, 'what's-happened-to-the-real-world?' sort of voice.)* Leonard . . .

THYNN: Yes?

74

A.P.: The prompter doesn't come on stage, Leonard. He stays out of sight, Leonard. He doesn't say 'Thynn's the name, prompting's the game,' Leonard. He doesn't say anything except little bits of lines to help the person who *is* on stage, Leonard. Are you sure you ought to be the prompter, Leonard?

THYNN: Well, I did it all right when I was in Miss Glanthorpe's play. *(Hastily.)* I know that was different, but—but I do want to be the prompter, I really do . . . I think I've got it now. I sit at the side of the stage, out of sight, and when people forget their lines I help them by calling out the next bit. How's that. *Let* me be . . .

A.P.: All right, Leonard. Okay, okay, okay, okay, okay! One more chance. Okay?

THYNN: Yep! Okay!

A.P.: Right. I'll use a different bit of the script, the bit that starts 'Down in the den . . . '—the narrator's bit. Got it?

THYNN: *(Frantic rustling of scripts.)* Err . . . got it!

A.P.: You sit on that chair. *Stay* on that chair!

THYNN: Fine—no problem . . .

A.P.: And I'll be Gerald addressing the giraffe from over here. Okay so far?

THYNN: Ace!

A.P.: Sure?

THYNN: Ace cubed!

A.P.: Here we go then. Last chance!

THYNN: *(Humbly.)* Last chance . . .

A.P.: Off we go then:
Down in the den on the bone-strewn floor,
Where the lost men scream and the lions roar,
Where a man whose gods are life and breath
Will lose his gods in the jaws of death
Where the strong alone . . . err . . . prompt!

75

THYNN: Will hold their creed . . .

A.P.: Where the strong alone will hold their creed, In the tearing grip of the . . . err . . . err . . . prompt!

THYNN: Lions' greed!

A.P.: In the tearing grip of the lions' greed . . . That's it, Leonard! You've done it! You've got it right!

THYNN: *(Clearly astounded.)* I have?

A.P.: That was perfect. Well done!

THYNN: So I *am* the prompter?

A.P.: You certainly are, Leonard.

THYNN: I really understand now, don't I?

A.P.: You really do! Well, I must fly, Leonard. I'll see you later. Thank your mother for the coffee. I haven't got much voice left. Bye!

THYNN: Yes, 'bye then! See you later . . . *(sound of doors opening and closing as A.P. leaves. After a few moments Thynn's voice can be heard in the kitchen as he speaks to his mother.)* Adrian said thank you for the coffee, mother!

MRS T.: 'E's welcome. 'Ow'd you get on with your wha'snamin'?

THYNN: Brilliant! I really understand it now. By the way, I hope you don't mind, but Adrian wants to borrow your big china giraffe for the evening of the performance. It's going to be the audience.

MRS T.: You'll 'ave to speak up, darlin'. I'm gettin' a bit deaf in me old age. I thought for a minute you said my big china giraffe was goin' to be the audience on the night of the play.

THYNN: I did say that, mother. It's the only bit I don't really understand. I've got to stay right out of sight in my soldier's uniform so that the giraffe can't see me when Percy Brain forgets his lines.

MRS T.: *(Suspiciously.)* You 'aven't bin back on the bottle again, 'ave you, Leonard?

THYNN: 'Course not, mother! I'm just telling you what Adrian told me. Apart from that, I understand everything perfectly . . .

MRS T.: That's nice, Leonard . . . 'Ave you switched your thing off?

[*Click! as Thynn rushes in to switch his machine off.*]

Four

Directing *Gandhi* would be simpler . . .

It wasn't until long after the performance of 'Daniel', that I heard the end of that third tape and realised why Thynn was so puzzled when he saw real people arriving to watch the performances at the drama festival. It also explained why he brought his three-foot-high china giraffe along and sat it in the middle of the front row. As soon as the seats started to fill up, his mighty brain must have realised the truth, because he went out and retrieved it. He stood it outside the men's toilet in the dressing room and said it was a mascot. The end of the tape also explains the origin of a persistent local rumour to the effect that the Home Secretary, Douglas Hurd, would be gracing the festival with his presence. I never did get round to asking the Thynns why they thought Mister Hurd was an appropriate name for a china giraffe. The way Leonard's mind works is one of the world's great unsolved mysteries. Still—he had got the hang of prompting, just about, so that was one more job done.

The next thing that happened was me getting neurotic about whether people had learned their lines or not. We only had time for two proper rehearsals before actually performing the thing, so it was essential that people had made a real stab at learning their parts. After all, no one had *that* much to say. Anne said I shouldn't phone people and check because I always end up in a bad temper; a gross exaggeration, but I thought it best to wait until she and Gerald were out. Unfortunately, they both came in with Thynn in tow just as I'd dialled Elsie's number and was waiting for someone to answer. When I told them what I was doing, Anne sighed, Gerald chuckled and Thynn whipped his ridiculous machine off his shoulder and stuck the microphone right next to the phone so that he could pick up both ends of the conversation. In some places I've put down what I *wanted* to say, in contrast with what I *did* say . . .

[*Click of recorder being switched on, followed by sound of receiver being picked up at the other end.*]

A.P.: (*With forced casualness.*) Hello, who's that?

ELSIE: (*For it is she.*) You don't think I'm stupid enough to give my name to potential telephone perverts, do you?

A.P.: I'm sorry, Elsie—it's Adrian Plass here.

ELSIE: I know, I recognised your voice.

A.P.: Well, why bother with all the telephone pervert stuff, then?

ELSIE: It's the principle. I'm training men.

A.P.: Oh, I see, well, consider me trained. Look here, Elsie, I'm ringing about your lines.

ELSIE: What lines?

A.P.: *What* lines? *Your* lines—in the play!

ELSIE: What play's that?

A.P.: (*With controlled but rapidly mounting fury.*) The play, Elsie! The Daniel play! The play we sat and talked about for goodness knows how long last Monday! The play we're doing at the Drama Festival. You *must* remember!

ELSIE: Oh, am I in that? Yes, I do remember

something vaguely about it. Well, you might have given me a script. It'll never be ready if you don't get the scripts out on time, will it?

A.P.: *(What I actually said, using massive self-control and Christian restraint.)* Elsie, my darling, I think you'll find, if you look, that I *have* sent you a script—some days ago, actually—and I really would be ever so grateful if you could just learn those four little lines by this Friday evening, which, as you'll see if you read the note I sent with the script, is when the first of our only two rehearsals is due to happen. So, as you can see, it really is important to get learning.

[*What I wanted to say while holding Elsie upside down over a vat of boiling oil)* You stupid egocentric, fluffy-haired twit of an adolescent! Why haven't you been eating and sleeping and breathing this play like I have, through every second of every minute of every hour of every day since I was foolish enough to start this whole horrendous exercise! And if, you empty-headed little ratbag, you haven't learned every single letter of every single word of every single line in your miserable little speech by Friday, I shall dunk you like a fancy biscuit into this boiling oil! Do I make myself clear?*]

ELSIE: Well, if you say you've sent it I suppose you must have. I'll try to glance at it before Friday if I get a moment. Wait a minute! Friday, did you say? William and I go out on Fridays. That's our night! *(With heavy reluctance.)* I suppose we *could* come out to this rehearsal of yours if we absolutely had to . . .

A.P.: *(What I actually said.)* I'd be so grateful if you could organise things so that it's possible to be there, Elsie.

[*What I wanted to say whilst waving a magnum pistol under her nose) Go ahead—don't turn up! Make my week, punk!*]

ELSIE: *(Sighing.)* I suppose I'll be there, then. Hold on a minute—William's here. He's saying something . . . *(Pause with distant muttering.)* William says he's got the smoke machine, and he's had lots more ideas about how to use it in the play.

A.P.: Oh, good, yes, that's err . . . good.

ELSIE: *(Powerfully.)* Mr Plass, I'm a Christian, so I forgive you freely for rejecting what I wrote as though it was a piece of rubbish, nor do I feel anger or resentment about your feeling that I look enough like a *boy* to be cast as a male servant! However, I would get very upset if I thought that William's creativity was being crushed.

A.P.: *(Sweetly.)* You've remembered an awful lot about the play suddenly, Elsie.

ELSIE: Yes—well . . . anyway, just as long as the most important person in the whole thing doesn't get . . .

A.P.: Meaning William?

ELSIE: Of course! Just as long as William doesn't get . . .

A.P.: Crushed . . .

ELSIE: Exactly!

A.P.: *(With superhuman control.)* I shall do my very best not to crush any aspect of William, Elsie.

ELSIE: Good! Well, I expect I'll see you on Friday, Mr Plass. I can't stay talking any longer. William's just bought a book about a man in the Solomon Islands who converted people by scratching their names on trees then laying hands on the bark. We're just going up to Hinkley Woods to do a few before suppertime. We thought we'd do it road by road until the whole town's done. It may be that there's time for us to look at the play later on this evening. We'll see.

A.P.: Thank you *very* much, Elsie. How *very* kind of you. Goodbye.

[*Sound of receiver being placed gently down, then ground viciously into its cradle.*]

ANNE: I don't know why you bother, darling. I told you you'd end up in a bad temper. Why don't you just leave them? They'll learn their lines all right. You get yourself in such a state!

A.P.: I am not in a state!

ANNE: You are, you've got those little white bits at the corners of your mouth. You're in a state!

GERALD: And you keep rubbing the back of your neck with your hand. You always do that when you're in a state.

THYNN: (*Suicidally.*) Say something into the microphone about being in a state.

[*Sound of vicious dialling.*]

ANNE: You're not ringing someone else, surely, Adrian. It'll only get worse, you know it will! Why don't you come and have a nice cup of tea and forget . . .

A.P.: (*Grim.*) Hello, is that Percy?—Get that microphone out of my nose, Leonard—Percy, I'm just checking that you've learned your lines okay . . .

PERCY: An actor prepares! I am engaged in all aspects of what promises to be a highly demanding role!

I have been soaking myself in historical and biblical references to kingship in ancient Babylon. I dwell within the skin of King Darius!

A.P.: Have you learned your lines, Percy?

PERCY: I shall proceed according to the tenets of the master, Stanislavski. I shall build a character upon the rock of my own personality. Layer upon layer, nuance upon nuance, like some insubstantial phantom slowly gaining flesh and blood reality, the person I am to become will emerge, and live!

A.P.: Have you learned your lines, Percy?

PERCY: I have delved deep into the very entrails of the *meaning* of the words, and I am discovering . . .

A.P.: Have you learned your lines, Percy?

PERCY: I am immersed in . . .

A.P.: Have you learned your lines, Percy?

PERCY: I have . . .

A.P.: Have you learned your lines, Percy?

PERCY: I . . .

A.P.: HAVE YOU LEARNED YOUR LINES, PERCY?

PERCY: No, I have not! I must not be troubled by such trivial details at this stage in my flow through the estuary of rehearsal towards the deep ocean of performance!

A.P.: You'll end up in the little dribble of not being in it, if you don't learn your lines, Percy. Do I make myself clear?

PERCY: *(After a little rumbling.)* Possibly the optimum moment has arrived for a little vulgar line-learning. Rest assured I shall err . . . attend to it. In fact, I shall err . . . attend to it now. Farewell!

A.P.: *(Through his teeth.)* Farewell, Percy!

[*Sound of phone slamming down.*]

GERALD: It's wonderful how you manage to stay cool, dad. You'd make a good nun.

THYNN: You've got the feet for it.

A.P.: What do you mean, I've got the feet for it?

THYNN: Well, you know those King peng . . .

ANNE: Darling, don't make any more calls—please! You'll end up marching up and down the hall blowing through your nose and muttering to yourself. Why not just leave it?

GERALD: Yeah, leave it, dad. You can trust Edwin to learn his lines, and you wouldn't have the nerve to ask Mrs Flushpool if she's learned her words, so . . .

ANNE: Gerald, you really are unbelievably silly sometimes!

[*More vicious dialling.*]

A.P.: (*Hums tensely as he waits.*) Hello, is that Vic—Leonard, I shall insert that microphone into you if you don't hold it away from my face—I'm sorry, is that Vict . . .

MRS F.: Who is that?

A.P.: Hello, Victoria, it's Adrian Plass here. I just phoned to ask you—(*Suddenly remembers the new 'be nice to MRS F.' decision*) to ask you err . . . how you are. (*Lamely.*) How are you?

MRS F.: (*A little taken aback.*) I am well, and rejoicing in my daily defeat of the natural. Today I have eschewed chiropody. My feet were a thorn in my flesh.

A.P.: Really . . . Good! Well, I also wanted to ask you err . . . (*nerve gone*) how Stenneth is.

MRS F.: Stenneth is seated at the pianoforté perusing

a new and most instructive book—*Sermons Set to Music*, by Doctor Martyn Lloyd Webber. He is quite content.

A.P.: Good, good! That's good . . .

MRS F.: Was there something else, Adrian? I am at present . . .

A.P.: There was just one thing—err . . . I wondered if you've yet managed to—to . . .

MRS F.: Yes?

A.P.: To err . . . to plan your holiday for next year.

MRS F.: We do not take holidays, Adrian. We do not *believe* in holidays. We undertake periods of recreational outreach.

A.P.: Ah, I see . . . well, where are you planning to err . . . undertake your period of recreational outreach next year?

MRS F.: Benidorm.

A.P.: Ah . . . yes, very commendable . . .

MRS F.: If there's nothing else, I really ought to get on with . . .

A.P.: *(Desperately.)* I really did just want to—to know . . .

[*Sound of Gerald making chicken noises in the background.*]

MRS F.: To know what?

A.P.: To know—to know err . . .

MRS F.: Adrian, I am engaged in the task of learning my lines for the forthcoming dramatic production. I should like to continue with this task if at all possible!

A.P.: Ah! Right! Fine! Good! Sorry! Of course! Yes! Goodbye! See you later . . .

MRS F.: God willing, yes. Goodbye.

[*Sound of A.P.'s telephone being dropped onto its cradle.*]

GERALD: Have you got anything you want to melt, mum? You could use dad's face.

ANNE: Be quiet, Gerald! She was in the middle of learning them, was she, darling?

A.P.: *(After inhaling long and deeply through his nose.)* Yes. She was in the middle of learning them, Anne. If you don't stop following me around with that infernal mechanical lollipop, Leonard, you'll be recording your own death rattle.

ANNE: Anyway, you've checked everyone now, darling, except Edwin, and Gerald's quite right in saying that you can trust Edwin. Don't you think so?

A.P.: *(Sounds of weary chair-sinking.)* Oh, yes, I'm sure Edwin will do his stuff. I dunno . . . it's hard work, this directing business.

GERALD: It's good practice for saying: 'Do I make myself clear', though, dad. You must've said that at least, ooh, let me see . . .

A.P.: Thank you so much for your chicken imitation while I was on the phone, Gerald. It was most helpful and encouraging. Now, if you don't mind I'm going to—wait a minute!

ANNE: *(Quite alarmed.)* What is it, Adrian? Why are you looking at Gerald like that?

A.P.: *(In slow, menacing tones.)* There's just one other person we haven't checked. Isn't there, Gerald?

GERALD: Is there, dad?

A.P.: Yes, Gerald. You! I forgot all about you. You've got about twenty lines to learn, haven't you?

GERALD: Err . . . yes, that's about right . . .

A.P.: So how are we doing, my little chicken imitator? How many of our lines have we learned since we got our script? Eh?

GERALD: *(Airily.)* Oh, I don't think it matters if you

don't learn a script word for word. As long as you get the general sense, that's all that really counts. I'll just fudge along and more or less busk it. The rhymes don't add that much to it after all, do they?

[*Short pre-eruptive silence.*]

ANNE: *(Aghast.)* Gerald! What . . . ?
A.P.: *(A murderously incredulous growl.)* Fudge along . . . ? More or less busk it . . . ? Rhymes don't add that much to it . . . ? I'll teach you whether it matters if you don't learn a script word for word!

[*Sound of banging and crashing as A.P. chases Gerald around the room.*]

GERALD: *(Sounding, appropriately, like someone undergoing the pain of a half-nelson.)* Only joking, dad! Only joking! Listen:

> Pain is sharper than remorse,
> Death more final than regret,
> Darius will mourn tonight,

But live his life, perhaps forget.
While Daniel faces fearful hurt,
Beneath the dark remorseless flood.
That flood of fear which runs before
The tearing down of flesh and blood.

I know all the rest as well! Really I do! Listen:

Down in the den on the . . .

A.P.: You know it? You've learned it? You've . . .

GERALD: Of course. Got it off pat more or less immediately.

A.P.: So you thought you'd just give my blood pressure a little exercise, did you? Thanks a lot!

[*Sound of door opening and slamming as A.P. stomps off into the hall.*]

ANNE: Honestly, Gerald. When will you learn?

GERALD: Sorry, mum. Just couldn't resist it (*Chuckles.*) Went up like a volcano, didn't he?

THYNN: What's he doing now?

ANNE: He'll be doing just what I said he'd end up doing—marching up and down the hall blowing through his nose and muttering to himself.

THYNN: (*Excitedly.*) I must get that on tape!

ANNE: I really wouldn't . . .

[*Door opens and slams shut as THYNN disappears into the hall. Muffled sounds of conflict end with a muffled cry, and abrupt silence as the recorder is either deliberately or accidentally switched off.*]

Five

An angel unaware

I didn't kill Thynn in the hall. I quenched him with a very heavy old army greatcoat which happened to switch his machine off at the same time. I must admit I was a little miffed. I was beginning to feel a bit ashamed of the whole exercise really, if I'm honest. I hadn't lost my temper so much or so badly for a long time, and it wasn't exactly bringing out the best in others either. The day after not killing Thynn I decided to pop round and see Bill Dove. Bill and Kitty Dove had been my favourite elderly couple for years. They were amazingly good at making things seem 'okay' again—especially Kitty. When she died nearly a year ago, I was very upset. Anne and I tried to get round to see Bill every week or so.

'The thing is, Bill,' I said, 'that we don't get all this conflict—or hardly any of it—in services or church meetings. People make an effort to get on with each other, and things go more or less smoothly. Perhaps it's a big mistake to do this sort of thing.'

Bill chuckled like he always does. 'That's the 'ole point, mate! 'Seasy ter be all lovey-dovey in church an' that, innit? Piece o' cake! Summink like this what your doin', well, ain't so easy to keep the old pretendin' up, is it? Little bit of aggro—little bit of sortin' out—do us all good. Find out what's 'appenin' behind the old crinkly smiles, eh?'

'I don't think there's much happening behind my crinkly smile, Bill,' I said dismally. 'I seem to spend all my time getting irritable and telling people off.'

'Yer know what Kitty'd say if she was 'ere now, doncher, mate?'

'What would she say, Bill?'

'First of all she'd say 'ave another doughnut, Adrian. Then she'd say 'ow good it was that you was takin' on somethin' like this for Jesus, an 'ow if 'e wants you to do it, 'e'll make sure it ends up right. But . . .'

He leaned forward and tapped me on the chest. ''is idea of endin' up right might not be the same as your idea of endin' up right! An' it 'asn't got to matter! With me?'

'Yes, Bill,' I said. 'I think I'm with you—I do miss Kitty sometimes, Bill.'

'So do I, mate,' said Bill, smiling and sighing, 'so do I . . .'

The first of our two rehearsals was planned for the following Friday. We booked Unity Hall specially for the purpose, and I arranged that the actors should come early, so that we could do some rather interesting warm-up exercises from a book I'd bought called *The Third Book of Theatrical Themes for Theological Thespians*. Nearly everybody was there on time. Gerald, Percy, Edwin, Charles, Vernon and Stenneth were all there by five past seven. Stenneth explained that Victoria would be a little late as she was in the middle of speaking to a neighbour about his son's musical excesses, but would get there as soon as she could. Thynn was there early as well, thinking he'd be allowed to sit on the side and laugh at us. I said he could only stay if he left his machine switched on and joined in properly. There was no sign of Elsie by the time we got started. Just before we began I reminded everybody—including Stenneth, who seemed terribly pleased—that we were going to make an extra special effort to be nice to Victoria starting from when she first walked through the door this evening. Everyone nodded enthusiastically and said they'd really have a go. This tape starts just as I began to explain the first warm-up exercise:

[*General murmur of conversation as people find a space on the floor of the hall.*]

A.P.: Right! If we could have a bit of hush we'll be able to get going. The first . . .

PERCY: I hope that these activities are well-advised! I feel in my bones that I should be curled in a corner balancing the brim-full container of character until rehearsal commences.

THYNN: He means he's not sure if he's learned his lines yet. He wants to grab a chance to . . .

PERCY: How dare you! I am word perfect! My method is . . .

EDWIN: Let's get on, shall we? I'm sure Percy knows his lines, Leonard.

A.P.: Thank you, Edwin, thank you very much. Now, the first of our exercises is designed to help us to—(*reads from book*) 'loosen up and lose inhibitions'. So I want everybody to come up this end of the hall and stand with your backs against the wall so that we're all facing the door at the other end. Right, off you go!

[*Clatter and nervous murmur as all move.*]

A.P.: Shush, everybody! Now, this might seem a bit strange, but I want us all to . . .

THYNN: Adrian?

A.P.: Yes, Leonard. What is it?

THYNN: Can I go to the toilet, please?

A.P.: Leonard, don't worry! I promise I won't make you do anything embarrassing—okay?

THYNN: We won't have to stand on boxes and do dances, or feel each other with blindfolds on or anything like that?

A.P.: No, nothing like that.

THYNN: Or one of us lie on the floor and the others stand round in a circle talking about him?

A.P.: No, Leonard!

GERALD: We *are* doing the one where we exchange clothes with the person we like least, while everyone watches, aren't we, dad?

THYNN: *(Panic stricken.)* I'm going to the boys' tiddler room!

A.P.: Come back, Leonard! Gerald was joking, *weren't* you, Gerald?

THYNN: *(Warily.)* Were you, Gerald?

GERALD: 'Course I was, Leonard. *(Blithely.)* Sorry, dad!

A.P.: If we were Russians, Gerald, I would be very tempted to show you where the crayfish spend the winter.

THYNN: Eh?

PERCY: I believe he meant . . .

A.P.: Never mind what I meant! Let's get on. Now, for our first exercise we're all going to shout as loud as we can down the hall.

CHARLES: *(Nervously.)* Err . . . ?

A.P.: Yes, Charles?

CHARLES: Err . . . I'm not really just err . . . clear about what we should err . . . shout . . .

A.P.: Well, the book suggests that everyone should shout, 'I hate you!' Sounds a bit funny, I know,

92

but that's what it says. The idea is we clear out all the repressed aggression and bad temper that's got stuck inside and pushed down and err . . . that sort of thing . . .

[*Blank silence for a couple of seconds.*]

THYNN: I'm going to the boys' tiddl . . .
A.P.: STAND STILL, LEONARD! No exercise— no uniform! Now, everybody, after three—one! two! thr . . .
CHARLES: *(In an abrupt reedy scream.)* I hate you!

[*Shocked silence.*]

A.P.: Yes, Charles. Err . . . good effort. If we could just try it together this time. Ready, everyone? One! Two! Three!
ALL: *(A pathetic, totally unaggressive mooing sound.)* I hate you . . .
VERNON: . . . in love.
A.P.: No, Vernon, we don't add 'in love', on the end. As for the rest of you, I don't honestly think an awful lot of aggression came out of us then, do you? Now come on, backs to the wall and really shout it out. After three again. One! Two! Three!
ALL: *(A faintly annoyed mooing sound.)* I hate you . . .
CHARLES: In l . . . sorry!
A.P.: Look, let's just try to imagine the person or thing we hate most, and then try again, right? Edwin, what would that be for you?
EDWIN: Hmmm . . . interesting. I think for me it would be the devil.

[*Impressed murmur.*]

93

A.P.: Good! Stenneth, what about you? Who do you hate most?

STENNETH: *(With passion.)* Those who wantonly destroy balsa-wood models without compunction!

A.P.: Err . . . yes, right—good one, Stenneth. Leonard, dare I ask?

THYNN: Me.

A.P.: Pardon.

THYNN: Me. I'm the one I hate most—especially when I'm drinking.

[*Embarrassed pause.*]

EDWIN: I don't hate you, Leonard—I love you. You're my friend. *(Slap of hand on shoulder.)* Charles, what about you? Who do you hate most?

CHARLES: *(Vaguely.)* Err . . . Joe Bugner I think . . .

A.P.: Why Joe Bugner?

CHARLES: I don't really know. I just really . . .

PERCY: Loneliness! For me it is accursed loneliness! That I can shout at. Loneliness . . .

A.P.: Well, I think we're really getting somewhere now. You see! Everyone's got something they'd like to have a shout at. Vernon, what's your pet hate?

VERNON: *(With wild intensity.)* I really hate it when you have a bath, then suddenly realise you've forgotten to bring a towel in, and you're staying in someone else's house, and you shout for someone to fetch one from your bedroom, then suddenly remember you've left your dirty old socks and a Biggles book lying around in your room and there's nothing else you can do and you want to die!

THYNN: Have you got *Biggles and the Little Green God,*

Vernon? That's the only one I haven't . . .

A.P.: Right, well I think that's everyone . . .

THYNN: Expostulated Algy . . .

A.P.: What?

THYNN: Opined Ginger . . .

A.P.: Do be quiet, Leonard.

THYNN: Voiced Bertie . . .

A.P.: Leonard!

THYNN: Encapsulated Biggles, as the air commodore pushed his cigarette box across the desk . . .

A.P.: Leonard, be quiet! *(Pause.)* Thank you. Now, we've all identified something or someone that we hate—right?

GERALD: Daddy, dear!

A.P.: *(Sighing.)* Sorry, Gerald. I forgot you. What do you hate most?

GERALD: *(Pathetically.)* Being left out by daddy-doos, I think.

A.P.: If you don't want to be left out altogether by daddy-doos, you'd better decide what you really hate most, Gerald.

GERALD: What, seriously?

A.P.: *(A little taken aback.)* Well, err . . . yes, seriously.

GERALD: *(After a short pause.)* Well, if you must know, I hate it when people think that just because I tell jokes and take the mickey sometimes it means I'm not serious about anything, or that I don't really believe in God, or that I'm just being nasty. I expect it's my fault sometimes, but . . . well that's what I really hate most . . .

A.P.: *(Quietly.)* Thank you, Gerald. *(Briskly.)* That's everyone, then. Let's . . .

THYNN: Err . . . excuse me, air-commodore?

A.P.: *(Testily.)* What now?

THYNN: You haven't told us what *you* hate most—interrogated Von Stalhein.

A.P.: Apart from ridiculous un-funny allusions to Biggles books, you mean?

THYNN: Sorry.

VERNON: Go on, Adrian, tell us who you hate most. We've all said ours, so it's sort of only really thingy, isn't it?

A.P.: Never let it be said that I am anything but thingy, Vernon! The thing I hate most, now let me see . . . I think probably one of the things I hate most is anyone being nasty to Anne. I can't stand that. *(Ruefully.)* I'm the only one who's allowed to be nasty to Anne. I didn't mean that I never err . . . you know. But I don't like it when someone else err . . . isn't—or rather—is being err . . . nasty.

EDWIN: I think that really is everyone now, Adrian.

A.P.: Good! Now, stand up straight—backs to the wall! After three. Think about all those things we've just said we hate so much! In fact, let's not shout '*I* hate you.' Let's shout '*We* hate you,' as loud as we can—really feel it together! Ready?

[*Chorus of agreement.*]

ALL: We hate you!

A.P.: Not bad! Not at all bad! But we can do even better! One, two, three!

ALL: *(With considerable volume.)* We hate you!!

A.P.: And again! Really let it go!

ALL: *(Quite caught up in it now.)* We hate you!!!

A.P.: One more time! One, two, three, go!!

ALL: *(A terrifying scream.)* WE HATE YOU!!!

[*Sound of a body slumping to the floor as MRS FLUSHPOOL collapses with the shock of seven people— including her husband—screaming hate at her as she comes in through the door at the opposite end of the hall.*)

A.P.: Oh, no! We were going to be specially . . .

[*Clatter of feet as everyone surround* MRS F. *and helps her to her feet.*]

CHARLES: (*Wildly.*) I wasn't shouting at you—I was shouting at Joe Bugner!

MRS F.: (*Faintly.*) What?

EDWIN: It was just an unfortunate coincidence, Victoria. As far as I was concerned, I was shouting at the dev—err . . . at somebody completely different. I do hope . . .

VERNON: (*Comfortingly.*) It was in love . . .

97

MRS F.: *(In high-pitched bewilderment.)* How can you scream at someone that you hate them *in love*?

VERNON: You don't understand, Mrs Flushpool. We were using our imaginations. I was pretending I'd got no clothes on.

MRS F.: An orgy! Stenneth, how could you?

STENNETH: *(Sounding like the captain of the Titanic surveying his future just after the impact.)* Victoria, words fail me . . .

A.P.: It's actually very simple to explain, Victoria. We were doing an exercise from a drama book I've bought. You get rid of aggression and stuff by shouting 'I hate you' as loudly as you can. That's what we were doing. You just happened to come in when we reached our err . . . peak, as it were. I'm awfully sorry. Please forgive us.

MRS F.: *(Graciously.)* In the natural you would certainly have found me intransigent. I hope that I am now capable of exercising reflective redemption.

THYNN: Yes, but are we forgiven?

EDWIN: That's what Victoria meant, Leonard.

STENNETH: So *I* am err . . . forgiven, Victoria?

MRS F.: Naturally, Stenneth. It is a scriptural obligation. I would, however, be extremely interested to know what your particular imaginary object of hatred happened to be.

STENNETH: *(The blood draining from his words.)* Of—of course, my dear. My err . . . main object of hatred was, well, it was actually err . . . it was . . . *(Looks imploringly at the the others.)* Henry the Eighth! Wasn't it, everybody?

EDWIN: Err . . . yes, I believe it was something like that, Stenneth, yes.

THYNN: *(Trying to be helpful.)* I thought it was Henry the Seventh . . .

A.P.: *(Firmly.)* It was Henry the Eighth, Leonard! Wasn't it, Gerald?

GERALD: Yes! Definitely! 'Enery the Eighth!

MRS F.: Very suitable I'm sure, Stenneth. A notorious bigamist.

A.P.: Perhaps if you're feeling okay now, Victoria, we could move on to the second exercise. What do you think?

MRS F.: That rather depends on what the second exercise *is*, Adrian. I will not wink at impropriety.

THYNN: Eh?

A.P.: It really is quite proper, Victoria. We simply sit in a circle and think peaceful thoughts, then share our mental images with others. It's the opposite of the first one if you like. Instead of thinking about the thing you hate most, you think about nice, beautiful things, things that make you feel happy and relaxed.

THYNN: *(Remembering the 'Be nice to MRS F.' vow and overdoing it as usual.)* Dear, sweet, kind Mrs Flushpool, do please be good enough to join us in this little tiny exercise. We shall be miserable and upset if your pretty face isn't there for all to see in our little circle in a moment.

MRS F.: *(Unexpectedly flattered by Thynn's nonsense.)* Well, of course, one wants to be co-operative. *(To A.P.)* You say we are to sit in a circle?

A.P.: Err . . . yes, if we could all just form a rough circle on the floor . . .

[*General commotion as everyone tries to form a circle. A minute passes.*]

EDWIN: I think that's about as near as we're going to get, Adrian—a sort of bulgy oval.

A.P.: Right, well, if we could all be quiet now, and just concentrate on something that makes us feel good . . .

[*Brief silence, broken only by Thynn sighing heavily.*]

A.P.: Could we just err . . . come back now, as it were? Any volunteers to start us off . . . ?

CHARLES: I could just . . .

A.P.: Okay, Charles, off you go.

CHARLES: Well, I just sort of pictured myself dying and being lifted up by two heavenly cherubims until I found that I had entered a city of gold, where I joined a white-robed throng singing praise and worship for all eternity to he who is above all and in all, and joy and elation filled the firmament!

A.P.: Wonderful! Leonard, what about you?

THYNN: (*Dreamily.*) I'm just starting my fifth pint of Theakston's Old Peculiar . . .

A.P.: Ah, right . . . err, Vernon?

VERNON: I was picturing a really huge auditorium full of people responding to a superb message from an internationally acclaimed evangelist and preacher.

A.P.: Who was the preacher?

VERNON: (*Modestly.*) Me.

[*Some laughter.*]

A.P.: No, no, fair enough. Better to be honest. Edwin? Were you imagining you were pope?

EDWIN: (*Laughing.*) I'm afraid mine was very boring. I was lying in the sun on a beautiful sandy beach, just listening to seagulls and seasidey sort of noises. Lovely. Not very holy I'm afraid . . .

GERALD: Mine isn't, either. I was only a blue, a pink and a black away from a hundred and forty-seven break. Steve Davis was sitting on his chair looking as sick as an interesting pig. *(Sighs.)* It was wonderful!

A.P.: It was a blooming miracle, seeing as the highest break you've ever scored is seventeen!

GERALD: Oh, come off it, dad! When we played at Frank Braddock's club I scored twenty-five points, and it would have been thirty-two if I hadn't mis-cued on the next black.

A.P.: Twenty-five points, my aunt! You mis-cued after seventeen points. I remember it as clearly as anything.

GERALD: That's good, coming from you. You're the only person I know who chalks up *after* a mis-cue!

A.P.: Well, who pushed his cue up his own nose when he was breaking off and trying to look professional and cool?

GERALD: Well, who said, 'Aren't the webs a problem?' when he was told there was a swan-necked spider on every table in the club?

A.P.: That was a joke, and you know it! I never thought . . .

EDWIN: *(Breaking in diplomatically.)* Adrian, you haven't told us what your err . . . beautiful thoughts were.

A.P.: What? Oh, right, sorry. Yes, err . . . actually I was just blank really. Quite serene, but blank, void, one of those empty pockets of . . .

GERALD: Now we're back to your snooker again.

A.P.: Sorry?

GERALD: Empty pockets . . .

A.P.: Now look, if you think . . .

STENNETH: *(Miles away, eyes still shut, suddenly speaks with a deep American accent.)* To boldly go where

101

no man has gone before . . . warp five if you please, Mr Sulu . . . beam me up, Scotty . . . what in hell's name *is* that, Mr Spock?

MRS F.: Stenneth!

STENNETH: *(Coming to with a start.)* Condition red! I mean err . . . yes, Captain—I mean, yes, Victoria.

GERALD: We can't imagine what you were thinking about, Stenneth.

[*General laughter.*]

STENNETH: *(Rather embarrassed.)* It used to be my— my favourite programme you see. I suppose it seemed so wonderfully adventurous and exciting. You never quite knew what was going to happen next, whereas . . .

MRS F.: Yes, Stenneth? Whereas what?

STENNETH: Whereas my own life *(hastily)*, although satisfactory in many ways, was somewhat err . . . predictable.

[*Pause as everyone waits for* MRS F. *to devour* STENNETH.]

MRS F.: *(Surprisingly subdued.)* I am aware, Stenneth, that your life is not, perhaps, as fulfilled and err . . . pleasant as it might be. I am also aware that I am not guiltless in respect of your occasional— your continual lack of contentment. I have been attempting since I first . . .

STENNETH: *(Genuinely distressed.)* Please, my dear, you mustn't . . .

MRS F.: Since I first undertook this role as an—angel, I have been attempting to imagine myself as such a being—with little success I am afraid. Just now

I was attempting to experience peace by picturing Stenneth and myself at our favourite places and activities—or rather, those activities that I assumed gave enjoyment to Stenneth despite never having asked him—and I was quite unable to properly relax. For some reason the challenge of having to present myself as an angel, a messenger from God, has made me realise something that I fear I have known for rather a long time. Namely, that, despite my redemption from the natural, I am consistently harsh and unpleasant to others, and—and I . . . oh, dear . . .

[*Sobs, sniffs and tissue-wielding sounds as* MRS F. *bursts into tears for the first time that any of us can remember.*]

STENNETH: Victoria, you're crying! Please don't cry, my dear . . .

THYNN: (*Kindhearted but wildly misguided.*) Don't cry, Mrs Flushpool. We don't think you're any of those things you said. We think you're the nicest, kindest, most wonderful person in the whole church! We think . . .

EDWIN: (*Taking over with that quiet authority he shows sometimes.*) No, Leonard—I know you're just trying to be kind, but that's not what's needed here. Victoria, you make me feel very humble. I only hope that I shall be able to reveal my negative side as openly as you have when my time comes. We forgive you fully for anything you've ever said or done that might have upset us, don't we, everybody?

[*Enthusiastic assent from all, especially Stenneth, nearly in tears himself.*]

EDWIN: And so will God, if we ask him. Do you want us to pray for a little while now before we go on with the rehearsal, Victoria.

MRS F.: *(Whispering.)* Yes, please — I would . . .

EDWIN: Okay, we will. Loving heavenly father, we pray—Leonard, is your machine over there recording?

THYNN: Yes, it is. Do you want me to . . . ?

EDWIN: Switch it off, there's a good chap.

[*Sound of footsteps, followed by a click! as the tape-recorder is switched off.*]

Six

Anne does the trick

It was quite right of Edwin to tell Leonard to switch
the tape-recorder off when we began praying with
Victoria. It was better kept private. But no one
remembered to switch it on again. I pretended to
commiserate with Leonard when we realised that the
whole of one rehearsal had gone unrecorded, but I
was quite glad really. It wasn't the line learning. I
was pleasantly surprised at how well everyone knew
their words. Leonard was quite upset to find that he
had hardly anything to do. We had a read-through
first, which went very well. It was the next bit that
got rather confusing. Perhaps I was trying to be just
a fraction more professional than I really am. I wanted
to use all the proper theatrical terms like they did in
*The Third Book of Theatrical Themes for Theological
Thespians*, but I made the mistake of not explaining
them properly first. With my eyes fixed on a series
of diagrams I'd drawn the night before, I called out
such a complicated barrage of instructions that, at one
point, everyone ended up in a bewildered huddle in
one corner of the hall and got annoyed with me.
Things got a lot easier after I explained what 'stage-
left', and 'up-stage' and 'stage-right' and 'down-stage'
actually mean. Percy already knew, of course, so did
Gerald, but the others took some time to absorb it
all. I was deeply thankful that Thynn wasn't part of

the acting team. He has a great deal of trouble sorting out left and right at the best of times.

The lions were a bit feeble at first. Then Gerald suggested they should imagine they were sitting in church, and that George Farmer had just reached that point in one of his twelve fruit-gum talks, when, after forty-five minutes, he says, 'That's a very important point, and I want to examine it more fully later . . .' After that they really put some aggression into their roaring. I had to stop Leonard roaring with them, but I sympathised—we all did.

Overall, the acting wasn't bad at all. Percy was a touch Knight-of-the-Theatre-ish, and Victoria tended to enter like the Fairy Godmother in Cinderella, but the standard seemed generally high, and by the time we finished everyone knew basically where to go and what to do. Gloria and Norma were there, sitting at the side and giggling when I got things wrong. Anne and Mrs Thynn came along later as well. Mrs Thynn assured me that she'd booked the lion costumes for our next rehearsal, and Norma was being very organised about all the other clothes, so that part of the arrangements seemed to be well looked after. Gloria said that the make-up was so simple that there was no point in doing it until the second rehearsal, which would have to be our dress-rehearsal as well. There was just one major problem. At the end of the rehearsal Anne came up and whispered the question that I'd been asking myself all evening: 'Darling, where on earth have Elsie and William got to?'

'I don't know!', I hissed, 'I wish I did. I asked Edwin where Elsie was earlier, but he said that as far as he knew they were coming. I could throttle her— fancy not coming at all!'

I grabbed Edwin just before he left, and asked him whether he was planning to quiz his daughter about

106

what was going on, but he smiled and said, 'Adrian, I'm going to annoy her intensely by appearing totally unconcerned about her absence tonight. I think she ought to sort it out with you—or you and Anne, perhaps.'

Later that weekend I phoned Elsie and asked as casually as I could (bearing in mind that I actually wanted to explode at her) whether she was planning to come to next Friday's rehearsal. There was a short pause, then she said, 'I suppose so, yes.' Conquering a temptation to swear loudly, I asked her if she could come half an hour early so that we could have a chat. She said, even more reluctantly, 'I suppose we could if we must, yes.' I said thank you quite calmly, then went into the garden and beat the hedge with a stick for a while.

The next Friday I felt quite nervous. Thynn didn't help much by arriving at the hall three-quarters of an hour early with his ever-present machine, very excited about the dress-rehearsal and especially about trying on the soldier's uniform that Norma had promised to get for him. I told him he'd have to clear off while Anne and I spoke to Elsie and William, so, grumbling a bit, he went off to buy a peach, and pester George Farmer in his fruit shop round the corner.

It was probably a good idea of Anne's that she should speak to the young couple on her own. She said that with the play on my mind, and feeling as angry as I did, I would degenerate into my Basil Fawlty mode within two minutes of starting the conversation. Neither of us realised that Leonard had left his machine switched on before he went out. Obviously we would have turned it off if we'd realised. I was quite amazed when Elsie agreed to allow this next bit to be included for publication. She's a good girl at heart, though.

I've started the transcription from when I left the hall 'to do something', and Anne settled down in the corner with Elsie and a very uneasy looking William.

ANNE: Elsie and William, you know why Adrian asked you to come early, don't you?

ELSIE: *(Defiantly.)* No!

WILLIAM: I suppose it's about . . .

ELSIE: William doesn't know why he did either.

ANNE: Is that right, William?

ELSIE: He doesn't . . .

ANNE: You do want William to tell the truth, don't you, Elsie?

ELSIE: *(Sulkily.)* Of course I do—I'm a Christian.

ANNE: Well then, William?

WILLIAM: Well, err . . . I suppose it's about why we didn't come along last Friday, is it?

[*Unconcerned sniff from Elsie.*]

ANNE: That's absolutely right. Adrian and all the others missed you ever so much on Friday evening. You're essential to the play and you just weren't there. We don't want to get angry with you, we just want to understand. Did you feel upset by anything that Adrian or anyone else said to you?

ELSIE: I was a tiny bit upset that my poems were turned down flat without any reason being given, and I don't quite understand why I'm a boy in this play, but as I told Mr Plass the other day, I'm a Christian, so I forgive him.

ANNE: You do?

ELSIE: Of course. I'm a . . .

ANNE: But that's not the reason you didn't come on Friday?

ELSIE: No, it's not. It's—tell Anne, William.

WILLIAM: *(Uncertainly.)* Yes, well, Elsie felt that . . .

ELSIE: *We* felt!

WILLIAM: *We* felt that err . . . well, that if it was meant to err . . . be err . . . well . . .

ELSIE: *(After loud throat-clearing.)* We felt that if God wanted this play to be performed he'd make sure it was all right on the night, and that we were being led to use our faith to believe that what we did would be all right without us having to let him down by doing it in our own strength, and—and . . .

WILLIAM: And there was a film on at the pictures that we'd been looking forward to, so . . .

ELSIE: *(Hastily and rather redly.)* It wasn't because of that! That was just a—coincidence. *(With more confidence.)* William and I had a time of prayer after tea on Friday and we really felt it was really right not to go to the rehearsal, didn't we, William?

WILLIAM: *(Unhappily.)* Well, you felt it first, and then—then I err . . . sort of did . . . I suppose . . . actually, I really wanted to go.

ANNE: To the rehearsal you mean?

WILLIAM: Yes, you see . . .

ELSIE: William!

WILLIAM: *(Eyes-shining sort of voice.)* . . . I don't know if Mr Plass mentioned it to you, but I've got one or two ideas about using smoke in this play. So, actually, I was quite keen to err . . . be there, but . . .

ANNE: But Elsie talked you out of it?

ELSIE: No, we *both* thought—I told you we had a prayer-time!

ANNE: Elsie, darling, do you remember when you were a very little girl and you had a yellow canary?

ELSIE: *(Surprised and not far away from tears.)* Yes . . . he was called Sammy . . .

ANNE: Do you remember when you went on holiday one summer, you came round to see me, and asked if I'd look after Sammy while you were away?

ELSIE: *(A small voice.)* Yes.

ANNE: You were very serious and very anxious, and you made me promise two or three times that I'd feed him every single day without fail until you came back. Remember, sweetheart?

ELSIE: Mmm, yes . . .

ANNE: But I bet you prayed every night while you were away that I wouldn't forget. Eh?

ELSIE: Yes, I used to screw my eyes tight shut and say 'Please, please, please, God!'

ANNE: And how was he when you did come back?

ELSIE: Fine—all right. He was all right, Anne.

ANNE: You didn't expect God to feed him while you were away, did you, love?

ELSIE: 'Course not . . .

ANNE: It's exactly the same with the play, Elsie. We've got to pray as if prayer's the only thing that works, and then work as if work's the only thing that works. I can't remember who said that, but I think it's true.

ELSIE: Mmm, well, perhaps . . .

ANNE: In any case—let's be honest—that wasn't the real problem, was it?

ELSIE: *(Very quietly.)* What do you mean?

ANNE: Well, you say you've forgiven Adrian for the things you felt hurt by, but it doesn't work automatically when you're a Christian. You have

110

to pray about it, think about it, do something
about it, and really *feel* it. You're still quite angry
about your poem not being used, and the other
thing, aren't you?

ELSIE: Well . . .

ANNE: Well?

ELSIE: Yes, I s'pose I am . . . *(Suddenly passionate.)*
I don't look like a boy! I don't, do I Anne?

ANNE: *(Laughing affectionately.)* No one ever said you
did, Elsie! If you must know—the reason Adrian
wanted you to be the servant was that he knew
once you were involved you'd put all your
enthusiasm into it. He just wanted you to be in
it. As for looking like a boy—well, do you want
to know what Adrian said to me when you
started going out with Gerald that time?

ELSIE: *(Avidly interested.)* Don't mind . . .

ANNE: He said, 'Trust Gerald to end up with a little
cracker like that.'

ELSIE: *(Blushingly pleased.)* Did he really say that?

ANNE: Would I lie to you, Elsie?

ELSIE: *(Simply.)* No, Anne, you don't tell lies. *(Pause.)*
Did he really say that?

WILLIAM: *(Inadvisedly incredulous.)* About Elsie?

ELSIE: William!

ANNE: And, let's face it, Elsie, you're not the only
one who had an idea turned down, are you?
There were Charles and Vernon and Percy and
Leonard, and even Gerald—although I don't
think he was very serious really.

[*Pause.*]

ELSIE: I've been a bit silly, haven't I?

ANNE: I think you owe William an apology, don't

111

you? He would have been here on Friday if it hadn't been for you, Elsie, wouldn't he?

[*Longer pause.*]

ELSIE: *(Reluctantly but bravely.)* Sorry, William, I was silly.

WILLIAM: *(Cheerfully.)* Does this mean it's full-steam ahead with the old smoke?

[*Sounds of me coming in through the door, trying to look as if I haven't been eavesdropping.*]

ADRIAN: I'm back! Everyone okay?

[*Sound of Elsie coming over and kissing me on the cheek.*]

ADRIAN: *(Terminally taken aback.)* What was that for?

ELSIE: It was a kiss from a little cracker. I'm sorry I wasn't there on Friday, Mr Plass, so is William, although it wasn't all his fault. But he is sorry, aren't you, William?

WILLIAM: Eh? Oh, yes! Now, let's talk smoke . . .

Anne certainly did the trick! Elsie couldn't have been more cheerful and enthusiastic than she was for the rest of that rehearsal. Just as well really; it was *very* hard work. Everyone came this time—the whole caboodle! There was Edwin and the rest of the actors, nervous but excited, Norma and Mrs Thynn complete with black clothes and lion costumes, Richard, fussing around with his cheque book asking about 'legitimately incurred expenses', and Gloria, armed with a box of make-up, towels, cleansing-cream and other intriguing tins and tubes. I felt quite nervous at the thought that this little crowd milling around noisily in the hall was relying on me to sort everything out. My confidence wasn't helped by the discovery, just as the last person had been made up and we were all ready to begin, that Thynn, after arriving three-quarters of an hour early, was now nowhere to be seen. He came rushing in after another five minutes (during which I didn't swear out loud because, as Elsie would say, I'm a Christian) clutching a big plastic bag full of George's apples, and shouting, 'Did you get my uniform, Norma?' You can trust Norma. Not only is she charming and pretty and, well . . . that sort of thing, but she never forgets a promise. Within a few minutes Leonard emerged from our little improvised changing room wearing the white uniform and plumed helmet of what I guessed to be something like a nineteenth century French colonial officer. The ideal costume for a prompter! He was overjoyed with it, and said it was an even better uniform than the one that Miss Glanthorpe had given him to wear.

The lions really didn't look too bad at all. The costumes were head-pieces with lion-like cloaks rather than complete cover-all affairs, so they didn't look as silly as they might have done. I'd paid a visit to the phantom of the opera a few days previously and managed to extract a sullen promise that the lions wouldn't be lit very brightly. I felt quite optimistic really, and a little ashamed of my doubts about Mrs Thynn's reliability. She said that the man in the costume hire shop told her he was hardly ever asked for his three lion costumes, so she'd decided to take them back tomorrow and re-hire them next Friday morning ready for the performance. That would make it cheaper. Richard nodded approvingly. So, like an idiot, did I, failing completely to register the significance of what Leonard's mother had said. A week later I was to remember her words only too well . . .

Meanwhile, the rehearsal started really well. They all seemed to be remembering lines and moves perfectly, until Percy's next to last speech in the final run-through.

PERCY: *(Sounding like a cross between Topol and Olivier.)* Servant of the living God . . . *(Pause.)*

THYNN: *(His first prompt of the evening.)* Hear my anguish.

PERCY: *(Irritably.)* I didn't need prompting, Leonard! That was a dramatic pause—a *planned* dramatic pause! *(To A.P..)* I shall commence my speech once more.

A.P.: All right, Percy, that's fine. From 'Servant of the living God', everybody. Leonard, don't prompt unless people really need it, okay?

THYNN: Well . . .

A.P.: Off you go, Percy.

PERCY: *(After throat-clearing.)*
Servant of the living God, hear my anguish!

[*Loud crunching noise as Thynn bites into one of his apples.*]

ALL: Ssh! Be quiet! Quiet! etc.

PERCY: *(Put off by Thynn's thunderous crunching.)* Has he kept his hand upon you in your danger? *(Long pause)* Err . . . *(Longer pause.)*

A.P.: Come on, Leonard! Prompt!

THYNN: *(After swallowing half an apple whole and nearly choking to death.)* Sorry! I thought it was another dramatic pause. Err . . . where are we? Oh, yes, right, here we are, Percy.
Does your God have power to—

114

PERCY: MAY I start my speech again, IF you please?
A.P.: *(Exasperated.)* Yes, yes! Off you go!

[*Another loud crunch as* THYNN *foolishly bites into a second apple.*]

PERCY: *(Determined to get it right this time.)*
Servant of the living God, hear my anguish,
Has he kept his hand upon you in your
    danger?
Does your God have power to rescue you from
    from danger?

Err . . . prompt!

THYNN: Drmnl smrnker mm . . .

PERCY: What?

THYNN: Danmnk sprklk mwe . . .

PERCY: I can't understand a word you're saying, Thynn!

THYNN: Dnml . . .

[*Sound of RICHARD COOK slapping THYNN suddenly and violently on the back, followed by cries of dismay and disgust as the members of the cast are showered with bits of half-chewed apple.*]

A.P.: Leonard, I think that, as a general rule, it's pretty safe to assume that apple-eating and prompting don't go together. What do you think?

THYNN: Err . . . yes, you could be right . . . *(coughing fit.)*

After that we got to the end of the run-through without any mishaps, and I got everyone to sit round in a circle for a last chat before we all went home. It said in *The Third Book of Theatrical Themes for Theological Thespians* that there was no point in saying anything that might lower confidence, so I was determined to be positive at all costs.

[*Hubbub of excited conversation.*]

A.P.: Right! If we could have a bit of hush . . .

[*Hubbub dies down gradually.*]

EDWIN: Shush, everybody! Adrian wants to talk to us.

A.P.: Thanks, Edwin. Err . . . all I really want to say is that you've all done amazingly well. I can't believe it's this good after just two rehearsals. Well done! I don't just mean the acting. I mean the costumes and the make-up and . . .

THYNN: The prompting.

A.P.: And the err . . . prompting, yes. Now, I've said all I want to say during the course of the evening, so it's over to you. Are there any questions?

MRS T.: We're *all* Christians, yer great goop!

THYNN: QUESTIONS, MOTHER!! ARE THERE ANY QUESTIONS!!

STENNETH: Err . . . I have a question.

A.P.: Yes, Stenneth?

STENNETH: I just wondered if it might be possible to keep our costumes when the production is over. I must confess I rather enjoy being a—a lion . . .

GERALD: Heh, good wheeze, Stenners! We could both roam the streets at night terrorising the locals with our bloodthirsty roars! What d'you say? We could eat Christians in the shopping precinct and . . .

A.P.: Thank you, Gerald. I'm sorry, Stenneth, but the costumes are only hired. I suppose you could always buy one if you wanted to err . . . use it at home.

GLORIA: I've got a leopard skin leotard at home, Stenneth, darling. We could get together and . . .

MRS F.: Err . . . could I just enquire, Adrian, whether you think my portrayal as err . . . an—an angel is, more or less err . . . satisfactory, or . . .

[*Amazing chorus of approval and praise from everyone else in the circle.*]

117

A.P.: Well, there's your answer, Victoria.

STENNETH: You're getting more like an angel every day, my dear, if I may say so.

NORMA: I agree, Victoria. It's been really lovely being with you this evening. You seem so sweet and relaxed.

THYNN: (*Goofily tactless.*) For a change.

[*Chorus of disapproval directed towards* THYNN *by everyone else in the circle.*]

MRS F.: No, no, Leonard is simply adhering to the truth. I do feel somehow—different. Perhaps there was more of the natural lodged in my personality than I realised . . .

ANNE: You *are* different, Victoria, and it's lovely. Something else, Adrian—what about William's smoke? We haven't actually seen any of it yet, have we?

WILLIAM: Ah, yes, well . . .

A.P.: William's going to—Carry on, William, you say.

WILLIAM: Adrian and I have agreed on a few places

A.P.: *Two* places!

WILLIAM: Err . . . yes, two places where loads of smoke . . .

A.P.: A *moderate* amount of smoke!

WILLIAM: Two places where a moderate amount of smoke would look really great!

PERCY: I hope that this smoke will not obscure any principal err . . . characters. Where are these two places?

WILLIAM: Well, one is . . .

A.P.: Nobody's going to be obscured, Percy. The first bit is just after Gerald's opening speech when we see the lions for the first time, and the second

118

one is after Victoria's angel speech, just before everything goes dark. Okay?

PERCY: That sounds reasonably satisfactory. I trust, by the way, that my performance was of a sufficiently high standard?

ANNE: *(Sensing the worry beneath Percy's casual question.)* Percy, you were quite as wonderful as I always thought you'd be. Your King Darius is a *real* king!

GLORIA: You're *marvellous*, Percy darling! Scrumptious! I could eat you!

VERNON: Yes, Charles and I think you're really great, Mr Brain!

CHARLES: Yes, just sort of really . . .

PERCY: *(Inflated beyond description now.)* Leonard? What do you think of my performance?

THYNN: Gorgeous, Percy, darling! Absolutely scrumptious! What do you think of my prompting, sweetheart?

[*Much amusement.*]

PERCY: *(Haughtily.)* Your prompting is singular, Leonard. I think that is the appropriate term—singular!

THYNN: Thank you, Percival. Wait a minute—what does singular mean?

A.P.: It means wonderful! Richard, are you happy with the way the money's going?

RICHARD: Our financial status is more than satisfactory, I'm very pleased to report. We are err . . . several aardvarks in hand, as it were.

GERALD: *(Who wasn't at the meeting where Richard revealed his dream.)* Several aardvarks in hand? Is this a new currency they introduced in the

middle of the night when I wasn't looking? Let
me guess how it goes:

Six wombats equal one aardvark.

Two aardvarks equal one wolverine.

Three wolverines equal one yak.

Five yaks equal one hairy mammoth.

Got change for a gibbon, dad? I need a jerbil
for the coffee machine. I reckon . . .

A.P.: Gerald, Richard was making a little joke about
. . .

CHARLES: *(Astonished.)* Did you really make a joke,
Father?

RICHARD: I was making a light-hearted reference to
a prophetic dream vouchsafed to me recently in
connection with the financial arrangements
pertaining to this production.

GERALD: *(Genuinely bewildered.)* About aardvarks?

RICHARD: Yes, I saw, as it were, a mighty herd of . . .

THYNN: Singular means only one, doesn't it? Very
observant of you to notice there's only one of
me, Percy. Well spotted!

PERCY: I did *not* mean that. I meant . . .

GERALD: What were they doing, Richard?

RICHARD: *(Solemnly.)* Flying in formation.

PERCY: I meant, Leonard, if you must know, that
your so-called prompting was execrable.

THYNN: Well, that's all right then!

[*Laughter.*]

GERALD: Tell us all about the aardvarks, Richard.

A.P.: *(Hastily.)* I think we're getting a bit off the point,
aren't we? Are there any more questions in
connection with the play?

ANNE: I'm sure we're all praying in a general sort of
way about what happens next Friday evening,

darling, but I wondered if it would be a good idea if Edwin just said a little prayer before we break up tonight.

A.P.: Sounds good to me. What does everyone else think?

ALL: Yes/Good idea/Mmm/Go for it, Edwin etc.

EDWIN: Okay—let's pray. *(Pauses.)* Dear Lord, I'm not much like Daniel—don't know how I'd get on with the lions, probably get eaten up, but I love you and I'd try to trust you. That's what I hope we all do next Friday—love you and try to trust you. We don't really know what success means, except that it's what you want. Look after us, Lord, keep us loving you and each other, and thanks for everything, past, present and future. In Jesus' name.

ALL: Amen.

[*Click! as Thynn switches his machine off.*]

Seven

Love a duck!

I didn't sleep much during the week leading up to the performance. Every night I lay awake imagining all the things that could possibly go wrong with 'Daniel in the Den'. On the Wednesday night I dreamed that Percy Brain dressed in a leopardskin leotard, and leading a pink aardvark on a chain, walked on to the stage, only to be crushed by a giant apple dropped by Thynn from somewhere up among the lighting bars. Turning to see what my neighbour in the audience thought about this, I found that I was sitting next to a King Penguin in evening dress who asked if he could borrow my feet. Then I woke up . . .

By Friday evening my nerves were so bad that Anne suggested I should ask Edwin to take charge backstage, so that, apart from going round to wish everybody good luck, I could just take my place with Anne in the audience and watch from the front. It was a good idea. Edwin never flaps. He seemed quite happy to take on this role when I phoned him, so that's the way we arranged it.

There were eight entries in the festival competition, four scheduled to appear before the interval, and four after. Ours was the one due immediately after the interval. The hall was packed by seven-twenty. Eight local churches were heavily represented, as well as the usual crowd come out of interest or curiosity. At the

122

back, seated behind a highly complex-looking control panel, sat the phantom of the opera surrounded by pieces of paper and sound cassettes. Somewhere among all that lot—I assumed—were our lighting requirements and a tape of lion roars, imitated with surprising success by William blowing through the outer covering of a matchbox.

At seven-twenty-eight Thynn emerged from the side door that led to the back-stage area, hurriedly scooped up a large china giraffe from a seat on the front row, and disappeared through the door again, much to the bewilderment of the giraffe's near-neighbours who'd been discussing its presence with great animation. At about seven-thirty-five, as the last few people straggled in and took their seats, the lights dimmed and Mr Lamberton-Pincney, who runs a group called 'Spot it and Stop it' in our church, stepped forward to begin his duties as Master of Ceremonies for the evening. I don't know how I sat still for that first half. The four offerings were worthy but dull, and seemed to go on for weeks. There wasn't a hint of humour in any of them—lots of death and repentance, and oodles of sad realisation. Ours wasn't a comedy either, of course, but at least there was a bit of drama and passion in it—and smoke! William was poised at the side of the phantom of the opera, ready for action when the time came. I began to feel quite hopeful.

At half-time the audience rose gratefully to pursue tea and biscuits, while I made my way backstage to see how everyone was getting on. They were all in one of the changing rooms, standing or sitting very tensely as though waiting for something. Thynn's machine was switched on.

[*Sound of door opening and closing as A.P. enters. Buzz of conversation stops abruptly.*]

A.P.: *(Brittle but bright.)* Hi, all! Everything okay?

VERNON: We've got a . . .

EDWIN: Everyone's made up who needs to be, Adrian. Gloria's done a great job, so that's all right. Gerald and Percy and Elsie and Victoria and I have all got our gear on, as you can see, and good old Leonard's all dressed up ready for the prompting, so we're ready to go just as soon as . . .

A.P.: *(Sensing disaster.)* As soon as what? What's gone wrong? Tell me!

[*Absolute uproar as everyone tries to speak at once.*]

EDWIN: *(Shouting.)* QUIET!

[*Silence.*]

A.P.: *(Tensely.)* Just tell me, Edwin—please!

EDWIN: It's just that—well, I might as well come straight out with it—the lion costumes haven't arrived yet.

A.P.: What?! Not arrived? They must have . . .

THYNN: Mother hasn't . . .

A.P.: Mother hasn't *what*? Somebody tell me!

[*More general uproar.*]

EDWIN: QUIET!!

[*Silence.*]

A.P.: Well?

EDWIN: Mrs Thynn hasn't arrived with the lion costumes yet. We've been waiting and waiting, thinking she'd turn up at any moment, but—well, I just don't know . . .

A.P.: But . . .

THYNN: She went into town this morning to do some shopping and get the costumes and things, and she said she'd see me at the hall this evening. I don't know where she is! I don't know what's happened to her! I don't know . . .

GLORIA: *(At her best.)* All right, Leonard, calm down now. It's all going to be okay. Come to Auntie Gloria . . .

CHARLES: Vernon's sort of just waiting . . .

EDWIN: I've sent Vernon out to wait by the back door so he can let us know if—I mean—*when* she appears.

A.P.: *(Panicking wildly.)* But there's only a few minutes before we're on! What do we do without lions? We can't go on with the play if . . .

[*Sound of door crashing open.*]

VERNON: She's coming!

[*Cries of relief and excitement.*]

GERALD: What about the costumes, Vernon?

VERNON: She's got a bundle under her arm. That must be them.

A.P.: Thank goodness for that! Do you want me to stay and . . .

EDWIN: *(Shooing me out.)* No, no, we'll be fine. You go back and sit out front. We'll sort it all out. Off you go! Relax and enjoy the show.

A.P.: Well, if you're sure . . .

EDWIN: Quite sure!

A.P.: *(At the door.)* Right, well, good luck, everyone! Good luck with the prompting, Leonard—and the recording.

THYNN: Yep! I'm going to switch it off now to make sure there's enough tape to record the actual . . .

[*Click! as Thynn switches off.*]

I can't describe the relief I felt as I went back to my seat and told Anne what had happened.

'Just think,' I said, 'after all this work, how close we came to disaster.'

'Yes, darling,' she replied, handing me a cold cup of tea, 'I'm sure we'll be okay now. It's very exciting, isn't it? All these people watching!'

It *was* exciting. As people started filing back to their seats I felt quite shivery with anticipation. It was when all but one or two of the audience were settled in their places, that Richard Cook suddenly appeared through the door I'd closed, rushed up to me, knelt by my chair and started whispering urgently in my ear.

'Edwin sent me to say that Mrs Thynn's brought the costumes!'

'I knew that!' I hissed back. 'You didn't have to come and tell me that!'

'Yes, but she hasn't brought the right costumes!'

'Well, it's too late to worry about that. Leopards, tigers, whatever they are, you'll just have to go ahead.'

'But you don't understand! Percy and Gerald are already up on stage behind the curtain and they don't know that the costumes are . . .

'Richard, the lights are going down. Mr Lamberton-Pincney will be introducing our play any second now! They'll just have to go ahead, understand?'

'Yes, but . . . '

'It's too late to worry, Richard!'

'But . . . '

'Sssh!'

As Richard scuttled off worriedly towards the

connecting door, the auditorium lights dimmed once more, and Mr Lamberton-Pincney's mournful, horse-like face was lit up by a spotlight shining on the curtains at the centre of the stage. In miserable, measured tones, he praised the offerings of the first half, and introduced the first play in the second part of the evening.

'Ladies and Gentlemen—Daniel in the Den!' As the curtains parted to reveal Percy standing majestically centre-stage, I felt a stab of pride and pleasure. He took two steps forward, moved a yard or two stage-right, then faced the audience and spoke in ringing tones. By now, Leonard had his recorder in position next to him, so the rest of the performance survives for posterity.

[*Sound of Percy's feet on the boards as he moves stage-right.*]

PERCY: Though ruling, ruled by men with hooded faces,
Jealous, not for me, but for their honoured places.
Lions indeed, made vicious not by hunger's pain,
But by their lust for power and selfish gain.
No darker hour than when I lightly penned
This blind agreement to destroy my servant-friend.
Within the veil of vanity my foolish eyes,
Perceived my greatness, but could not perceive their lies.
Oh, God of Daniel, guard your son tonight,
Do not defend the law, defend the right.
No sleep for me, no calm, no peace, no rest,

> For I have sanctified the worst, and sacrificed
>> the best.

GERALD: *(Entering stage-left)*
> Pain is sharper than remorse,
> Death more final than regret,
> Darius will mourn tonight,
> But live his life, perhaps forget
> While Daniel faces fearful hurt,
> Beneath the dark remorseless flood
> That . . . err . . .

THYNN: *(Prompting perfectly.)* That flood of fear
. . .

GERALD: That flood of fear which runs before
> The tearing down of flesh and blood.

It was marvellous! The opening speeches had been
superb, despite Gerald's lapse of memory, which,
thanks to Thynn, was hardly noticed. Now it was time
for William's first opportunity to use his beloved
smoke-machine. And he certainly used it! Despite my
constant pleas for moderation, within two minutes the
stage was completely filled with thick, impenetrable,
yellow smoke. Percy and Gerald, their backs to the
audience, peered hopelessly into the swirling mist,
waiting for the lions to appear. The moment when
the smoke cleared at last, and three large pantomime
ducks waddled forward from the back of the stage will
stay in my memory until the day I die. Percy was
completely transfixed. From my place at the end of
a row I could see his jaw hanging slackly down, his
eyes wide and staring as the absurdly costumed trio
tried to look menacing. A ripple of laughter passed
through the audience as the ducks first hove into view,
building to loud, uncontrollable guffaws, as they
started to growl softly.

Gerald recovered first. Turning back towards the audience he gathered himself together, and delivered the following on-the-spot adaptation of his second speech.

GERALD: Down in the den where it's dark and black,
Where the lost men scream and the ducks go quack
Where a man whose gods are life and breath,
Will lose his gods in the beak of death.

[*Shouts of laughter.*]

Where the weak will lose their sworn religion,
In the tearing grip of a pin-tailed widgeon.

[*Screams of laughter.*]

THYNN: (*Audible to the mike, but not the audience.*) That's not what it says here!

PERCY: (*Recovering like the old trouper he is.*)
Oh, Daniel, Daniel save me from my madness,
Pray your God's compassion on my sadness,
Bid him send an all-forgiving rain,
To wash these excess mallards down the drain.

ELSIE: (*Entering stage left and getting the idea immediately.*)
I wait upon you master as you bade me wait,
To bring intelligence of Daniel and his fate.
Some moments past your man, of whom you're fond,
Was taken out and thrown into the pond.

PERCY: Save him God, hear my appeal!
Save him for that flock of teal!

129

THYNN: *(Louder.)* That's not what it says here!
*(Wanders out onto the stage absent-mindedly, studying
his script.)* That's not what it says here, Percy!
There's nothing about ducks!

[*Wild laughter from the audience on seeing someone in
a nineteenth-century French colonial officer's uniform
wandering inexplicably around the stage among the
ducks.*]

STENNETH: *(A muffled bleat through his duck head.)* She
brought the wrong costumes, Leonard! She
brought ducks!

GERALD: *(Pushing between STENNETH DUCK and THYNN to
address the audience.)*
    Now the moment, now the test,
    See Jehovah's servant blessed,
    Standing here with troubled scowl
    Before these deadly water-fowl.

Glad to earn the highest crown,
By ending up in eiderdown.

[*Loud roars from the speakers as the 'phantom' puts on William's tape. Audience collapses again as the ducks bob up and down, opening and shutting their beaks in time with the roars.*]

THYNN: (*Wildly at centre-stage.*) You're all getting it wrong! There aren't any ducks in it!
EDWIN: (*Entering stage-left.*)
    Though I may be short of pluck
    I'm not afraid to face a duck!
    I'll cut these creatures into thirds,
    The stupid geriatric birds!
THYNN: (*Very indignant.*) That's *completely* wrong!
MRS F.: (*Entering stage-right with a very straight, severe face. Touches each duck's head in turn with her hand.*)
    Here they lie, those mighty killers,
    Harmless where great harm has been,
    Sleep, and when the dawn has risen,
    Tell the king what you have seen.
    (*Moves over and touches Edwin's head with her hand.*)
    Daniel, you *shall* go to the ball!

[*MRS FLUSHPOOL'S face suddenly cracks into a real smile and she laughs until she cries.*]

THYNN: (*Resting his arm on VERNON DUCK'S shoulder.*)
    Now that *is* wrong!
GERALD: If you would score, you mighty kings,
    Be sure, don't trust to luck.
    If you don't score by God's own law,
    You'll end up with a duck.
THYNN: That's not . . . !
GERALD: Come on, everyone!

131

[*Gerald gets all on stage into a chorus line, and leads them into song.*]

ALL: Knees up Daniel Brown!
             Knees up Daniel Brown!
             Knees up! Knees up!
             Better get your knees up,
             Knees up Daniel Brown! Oi!

THYNN: We never sung that at rehearsals . . .

At this point the phantom of the opera, knowing that he was supposed to black out the stage somewhere in the course of the action, decided that now would be as good a time as any. Who can blame him?

When the lights came back on, the cast of 'Daniel in the Ducks' Den' received the only standing ovation ever witnessed in that building. People cheered and clapped for a good three or four minutes, while the actors waved and bowed extravagantly until the applause died down. Thynn, postponing his quest for some basic understanding of what was going on, waved and bowed with the rest, a blank but happy grin stretched across his face.

I felt sorry for the people in the three plays that came after ours. Two of them were quite good, but there was no doubt about it—nothing, on this particular night, was going to match the emergence of those three ducks from the middle of William's smoke. I think I had experienced every emotion known to man during the 'Daniel' performance, and as I joined in the applause for the final offering of the evening I felt quite exhausted. Four more significant things were yet to happen, though, before we left for home that night.

First, Mr Lamberton-Pincney announced immediately after the final play had finished that the judges' overwhelming and unanimous decision was

132

that 'Daniel in the Den' was the winning entry, and I was called up on stage to collect the little silver cup on behalf of our church, for a 'hilarious and cleverly devised comedy'. Feeling terribly guilty, I tried to explain to Mr Lamberton-Pincney and the audience that our play was meant to be serious and had only become funny by accident. The more I tried to explain, though, the more they obviously thought I was being terribly witty. They just laughed and clapped. In the end I gave up, and decided to explain to whoever was in charge later on.

The next thing was that Anne, who'd nearly died of laughing from 'ducks' onwards, steered me through the crowds of lingering theatre-goers to where a little old lady was sitting next to Leonard, still in his uniform and clutching Mr Hurd. They were chatting away like mad.

'Miss Glanthorpe,' whispered Anne in my ear. 'A little surprise I organised. Found her in the book. She's eighty-two!'

I looked at Anne for a moment, then moved closer to eavesdrop.

'You were absolutely marvellous, Leonard,' Miss Glanthorpe was saying, her little eyes twinkling as she surveyed the white-clad figure.

Leonard beamed happily.

'I don't quite understand though,' went on the old lady, 'the significance of this splendid uniform, and I was just wondering why you have that big china giraffe sitting on your knee . . . '

'Oh, that's easy to explain,' said Leonard confidently, 'I was wearing uniform because I was the prompter, and I was supposed to stay out of sight so that the giraffe couldn't see me when Percy Brain forgot his lines.'

'I see, dear. How silly of me to be so dense.' The

little eyes twinkled even more. 'You know, Leonard . . . ?'

'Yes, Miss Glanthorpe?'

'You really haven't changed at all . . .'

The third thing was that as we moved away towards the backstage area we almost collided with Frank Braddock, our neighbour, and author of the play we'd just mangled. He was with Father John, an old friend of his, and an occasional very welcome guest speaker at our church.

'Frank,' I said apologetically, 'I just don't know what to say. I'm so . . .'

'Don't apologise!' boomed Frank taking his unlit pipe out of his mouth. 'I was just saying to old Bungles here that I haven't enjoyed anything so much in years. The moment when old Thynn wandered on in his uniform was just—I dunno, I could've died! My version was much more boring than yours.'

'It's nice of you to say that, Frank,' I replied gratefully, 'but it wasn't exactly what I set out to do. Winning was an accident. I can't really see this evening as a success, not really.'

'Not a success?' Father John broke in gently. 'Adrian, I've never seen Victoria Flushpool as she was on that stage this evening. Her eyes shone, she was laughing, she was part of you all. She's different. I wouldn't be at all surprised if the experience of rubbing up against each other in a real, side-by-side effort like this had changed all of you in one way or another. It all depends whose success you're talking about, you know. I sometimes think that football teams and dramatic societies might be just as important as prayer-meetings and Bible-studies . . .'

'Come on, Bungles!' Frank slapped his friend on the back. 'Enough deep stuff! We've just got time for a pint if we're quick . . .'

The fourth and last thing to happen was finding the cast and crew of 'Daniel in the Den', still sitting in the changing room behind the stage. Thynn followed Anne and me through the door as we went in, and stood leaning against the wall cuddling his giraffe. All conversation stopped as soon as I appeared, and they all stared at me, waiting to see what I'd say. I thought of what Father John had said as I looked round at the familiar faces. Vernon and Charles, as earnest as ever, had little frowns beneath hair still lank from being enclosed in hot costumes. Victoria and Stenneth were sitting closer together than usual—they seemed lighter somehow. Gerald looked the same as ever, leaning on the radiator and giving me a little quizzical smile. I suddenly realised how grown up he was getting. Richard was sitting on an old, burst horse-hair sofa, jammed in tightly by Gloria on one side and Norma on the other. William and Elsie sat cross-legged on the floor gazing up at me. They looked even younger than usual. Percy was in the only armchair, legs crossed stylishly, head thrown back, but watching me with wide eyes. Mrs Thynn was doing something busily with a piece of cloth held in her fingers. Her eyes darted up to meet mine every few seconds. Edwin was standing by the window looking as serene as ever. Anne stood very still beside me. There was someone else there as well, right in the middle of us, the one who decides what success really means.

'Those ducks!' I said, and we all burst into laughter at the same moment.

Other Marshall Pickering paperbacks

THE GROWING UP PAINS OF ADRIAN PLASS

Adrian Plass

When TV viewers in the south tune into 'Company', they can eavesdrop on a few friends enjoying some late night conversation around a kitchen table. For Adrian Plass, the programme is a landmark in his Christian life. With disarming frankness and irresistible humour, he unfolds his own story and that of some of the programme's memorable guests, such as David Watson, cleaning lady Jo Williams and Auschwitz survivor, Rabbi Hugo Grynn.

THE SACRED DIARY OF ADRIAN PLASS AGED 37¾
Illustrated by Dan Donovan

Adrian Plass

A full-length, slide-splitting paperback based on the hilarious diary entries in Christian Family magazine of Adrian Plass, 'an amiable but somewhat inept Christian'. By his own confession, Adrian 'makes many mistakes and is easily confused', but a reasssuring sense of belonging to the family of God is the solid, underlying theme.

OFF THE CHURCH WALL

Rob Portlock

A hilarious collection of cartoons by Rob Portlock, depicting the unusual ways in which people choose to behave in church!

THE HORIZONTAL EPISTLES OF ANDROMEDA VEAL
Illustrated by Dan Donovan

Adrian Plass

Adrian Plass, diary-writer *sans pareil* returns! This time he finds much to amuse him in the letters of Andromeda Veal, precocious eleven year old daughter of a Greenham woman, and shrewd commentator on her local church and the wider world.

Andromeda is in hospital with an undisclosed complaint. She seizes her chance to write all those letters that had to wait before – to, 'Gorgeous Chops', 'Ray Gun', 'Rabbit' Runcie, the Pope, and even Cliff Richard.

At the same time her friends of Sacred Diary fame write to her: Gerald with his mysterious 'persunnul problem', Mrs. Flushpool, Leonard Thynn, and also the local MP who vows that she 'can be sick in our hands'! She is also the lucky recipient of letters from conscientious Bible student Charles Cooke who finds 15 texts for every word of 'I hope you get better soon', and a large Christian organization whose aims appear to change from letter to letter. Of course Andromeda's illness gives her a chance to think more seriously about God too, even to the extent of writing him a letter.

All of this is interspersed with new diary entries from Adrian Plass' inimitable diary writer and Dan Donovan's hilarious illustrations.